A Whole New World

Great insights
into transformation
and righteousness

The Gospel
of Matthew

John Blackwell

Morgan James Publishing • NEW YORK

A Whole New World
The Gospel of Matthew

ISBN: 978-1-60037-846-1 (Paperback)
Library of Congress Control Number: 2010933818

Published by:
MORGAN JAMES PUBLISHING
1225 Franklin Ave Ste 32
Garden City, NY 11530-1693
Toll Free 800-485-4943
www.MorganJamesPublishing.com

Cover/Interior Design by:
Rachel Lopez
rachel@r2cdesign.com

Dedication

To Ben and Kathee Christensen

With Gratitude

Table of Contents

Foreword

BY MOLLY VETTER

I'M EXCITED ABOUT THIS BOOK BECAUSE IT does something I love: it connects the life-giving power at work in Jesus' resurrection with the world-transforming work toward justice. At a time when it's easier to see things in simplified polarities, this book invites us to come on a journey deeper into the complexities of Matthew's gospel.

John Blackwell has never been particularly drawn to small talk. For the several years when we served as pastors on a church staff together in San Diego, he was infamous for his consistency in steering lunchtime conversations away from small talk and deep into "big idea" territory. This book shows the best of how he does that: by using real stories of life—family, ministry, school—as occasions for considering important, big ideas.

This particular book, then, defies the unhelpful temptation toward expected dichotomy. With an approach that is theoretical and practical, complex and clear, John shows how the saving work of Jesus Christ connects integrally with work for justice and righteousness today. This connection lies at the heart of my passion for ministry. I've been blessed to experience this connection over and over: In breaking bread together with diverse neighbors at our free neighborhood meal, I find my congregation sharing something sacramental. In offering handmade blankets and shawls as gifts to a camp full of adults living with HIV/AIDS, I've understood something about the unlikely and beautiful reign of God that Jesus spoke into being with his beatitudes.

I hope that, in reading this book, you feel the energizing gift of the mystery it describes so clearly and accessibly: the power of a Gospel that invites us to embody Christ's salvation as we live well (righteously, to borrow John's language) in the world.

My sense is that we're hungry for this connection: for a reminder that our Christian faith compels us to live differently in the world by allowing us to be living vessels of the salvation we proclaim. By living the righteousness that John points us toward in this exploration of Matthew's gospel, we find ourselves daring to care about people living in poverty, people marginalized by our culture, people easily forgotten and overlooked in our world. We find ourselves empowered to respond to violence with creative, life-giving, loving acts. We dare to imagine that new ways of living with each other and creation are really possible. May it be so.

Chapter 1
before text messaging

The new form of insight can perhaps best be called Undivided Wholeness in Flowing Movement.

—DAVID BOHM, *Wholeness and the Implicate Order*

Do not store up for yourselves treasures on earth, where moth and rust consume and where thieves break in and steal; but store up for yourselves treasures in heaven, where neither moth nor rust consumes and where thieves do not break in and steal. For where your treasure is, there your heart will be also.

—JESUS, in Matthew 6:19–21 (*NRSV*)

My students live in a culture that communicates by means of text messages. There are many things that text messaging is good for. I myself use it (especially when I want to send brief announcements to my students!). But text messaging as a means of communication has its downside: Because communication is chopped up and fragmented, the information can also be.

Many of these same students have grown up in a Christian culture that quotes the Bible one verse at a time. This way of reading the Bible fits hand-in-glove with the world of text messaging. The consequence is that many of my students are surprised at how challenging the study of the Bible can be. They freely admit that they like for things to be simple and straightforward. Few come to a university-level class having thought about a single book of the Bible taken as a whole. How, for example, do the stories in a particular Gospel work together as a complete whole?

At the beginning of the semester, I try to prepare my students for the challenge by tuning them into the complexity of the Gospels. I use the term *complexity* with deliberation. I do *not* mean that the Gospels are complicated. The Gospels are *not* messy or chaotic. Nor do I think that a person has to be a specialist to unravel their mysteries. Any thoughtful person can take the plunge. But a word to the wise: It takes time—lots of it. The Gospels have to be read, reread, and then read yet again. Analysis can help, but only to a point. Mere analysis has its limits. Understanding the Gospels is like understanding a friend. A friendship that is based on analysis is no friendship at all. Genuine friendship involves knowing a person as that person is willing to be known. This requires kindness and respect. It takes time for a friendship to develop and grow. It can't be forced: Good friends need time alone, and good friendship cannot be possessive, demanding, or clingy. Friendship definitely requires commitment and faithfulness. A relationship where one person has an eye to discrediting the other in a covert game of *Gotcha* isn't friendship, but betrayal.

Once the friendship begins to unfold, we discover the friend to be wonderfully complex. No two friendships are alike because no two friends are alike. Nor is one friend completely the same from one day to the next. Friendship enriches us in beauty, and the beauty is directly related to the wonder of our friend's concrete, mysterious complexity. The reward is a friendship that is rich in interest. And as the relationship matures, its richness grows.

I find it helpful to approach the Gospels as I would a friend. I am interested in knowing the Gospels as they want to be known, by which I mean that I want to experience the Gospels as the Gospel writer wants the particular Gospel to be experienced. For me, this involves approaching the mystery which each Gospel writer conveys with respect and love. This works best if I set aside my presuppositions about a particular Gospel. If I approach the Gospel of Matthew thinking that I already have Matthew figured out, or worse, if I approach Matthew with an idea, theory, or formula that I will use Matthew to legitimate or to enforce, I am simply using Matthew's Gospel for premeditated purposes. Moreover, my purposes may not have anything to do with Matthew's. If, on the other hand, I am to embrace the wonder of Matthew's Gospel on Matthew's terms, it helps if I am prepared to embrace Matthew's own uniqueness and complexity. Again, the Gospels are not complicated, but neither are they always an easy read. And if (and this is a huge *if*) I am willing to hunker down and dig in, the rewards are, well, like a treasure hidden in a field (Matthew gets the credit for this one). And the treasure (if I might be so bold) includes insight, meaning, and encounters with immeasurable mystery.

This, at least, is my experience. This is also what my students almost always find surprising: They don't typically anticipate the Gospels' complexity. Nor do they look for the ways the stories in a particular Gospel unfold and work together. I am pleased that most students come to the college level study of the Bible in search of a better understanding of the Word of God. And I am most pleased if my class in some way satisfies this longing. But it is a rare student who anticipates that the Word is concretely embodied in a mysterious complex of artistic beauty. Because this idea is so alien to the students' thinking, I try to help them with analogies. My reason for this is simple: Jesus used analogies, and so do Matthew, Mark, Luke, and John.

The most helpful analogy that I can muster involves the human body. A human being is the mysterious embodiment of unique beauty. Each of us is a wondrous blending of systems (skeletal, gastro-intestinal, cardio-vascular, pulmonary, endocrine, neurological, reproductive, and the like), which are wed to human will, dispositions, propensities, thought patterns, modes of interaction, prejudices, viewpoints, habits, and so on. Human beauty is in large part the result of our complexity. Each of us embodies incalculable dignity. Our worth isn't a commodity: It isn't possible to place a price tag on a person. Our dignity, goodness, and beauty are of a completely different kind of value than what can be represented by money. This is why we know slavery, servitude, or genocide to be not only wrong, but absolutely so: They constitute a deadly assault on human dignity. Moreover, our deepest intuition recognizes human dignity as completely sovereign.

Because our dignity is a sovereign complex, no person can be reduced to a single aspect of our humanity. Each of us embodies a complex set of characteristics that, taken *together*, make up who we are.

Perhaps an even more simple analogy will illustrate the nature of this complex beauty: Her name was Daisy. Until December 2006, Daisy was our daughter Jaime's dog. In dog years, Daisy lived to the age of one hundred twelve. Owing to the pain of cancer, along with deafness and blindness, we finally had to ask our veterinarian to put her down. The joy that Daisy brought to our family in general and to Jaime in particular will never be replicated. We adopted Daisy from the Humane Society when she was about a year old (this time, I refer to human years). We hadn't had Daisy too very long before we recognized that her previous owner was abusive. Daisy was docile and submissive beyond what seemed normal to Nancy, Jaime, Dave (our son), and me. But equally clear was that Daisy loved the Blackwells, and she worshiped Jaime. Our delight was the gift of Daisy's unmistakable happiness, to which I must add Daisy's peculiar idiosyncrasies. To almost any command, Daisy would lie down. Her bark combined aspects of the howl of a coyote with the voice of cartoon character Scooby-Doo. Ask Daisy, "You wanna go bye-bye?" and she would bark, howl, and run in circles. When you took Daisy for a walk, her monomaniacal pleasure was so intense that she would pull on the leash, causing her throat to issue gurgling sounds that, were they to emanate from a human, would cause one to wonder if the administration of the Heimlich Maneuver were called for.

Our joy with Daisy led all of us to hope that we brought Daisy as much happiness as she brought us. I am convinced that when she was around Jaime, Daisy knew pure bliss.

This experience of Daisy's life and beauty led me to commission a painting of Daisy, which we would give to Jaime as a gift. The idea came to me not only because of our daughter's love of her dog's unique beauty, but also because Jaime's love was matched by the love and skill of an artist. Her name is Kay Hakoda, and I asked Kay if she would accept a commission to paint a portrait of Daisy. I was in no way surprised that Kay accepted. In addition to giving Kay more than a dozen photographs of Daisy, I also spent time describing her. Kay took the photos and spent time reflecting. She finally decided to work from one that Jaime took of Daisy sitting at Jaime's feet. After careful thought, Kay selected her palate and over the next couple of weeks created a painting that not only portrayed Daisy sitting at Jaime's bare foot, but also captured the wonder of Daisy's personality and charm. When we look at Kay's painting, we feel Daisy's liveliness.

What makes the painting so remarkable for us is that its beauty is the effect not only of the complexity of Kay's artistic insight, but also her love, joy, and endearing humility. For the Blackwells, the work of Kay Hakoda is the perfect capstone to Daisy's life of loyalty and love.

I use the analogy of the creating of this painting to help us understand the beauty of the Gospels because Matthew, Mark, Luke, and John are uniquely rich in their complex insight into the life, death, and resurrection of Jesus. Moreover, the Gospels, in their unique concreteness, draw us close to the mystery in which Jesus lived and with which God raised him from the dead. They make us witnesses not only to the way in which the power of God dwelt in Jesus, but also the way in which that same power dwells in the concrete realities of the world and circumstances in which we live.

Another analogy from the world of art will help me convey this idea. In the Tate Modern Museum of Art in London hangs a work by Gerhard Richter (b. 1932), entitled "Abstract Painting." Richter began his work with a brightly colored, red composition, which he divided vertically into four sections. He drew the paint across the canvass, using long batons, which were edged in flexible plastic. Richter then painted over the first layer, scraping and scratching in to the surface. This destroyed the first composition and created a new painting.

The "meaning" of this painting lies less in what it represents, or "says," and more in the effect that it has on us as we take it in. In Richter's own words, it helps us to "visualize a reality which we can neither see nor describe, but which we may nevertheless conclude to exist." Standing before this painting, we have the experience of sensing the presence of unseen realities which lie just beneath the surface. In other words, the effect of the painting on the viewer is to help us to sense the presence of unseen reality that, although invisible, is nonetheless present and embodied in the painting.

It is hard for me to imagine a better description of the effect of the four Gospels, including Matthew. He makes it possible for us to visualize not only the life, death, and resurrection of Christ, but also his affects and his effects in our own limited, concrete lives. Matthew makes us witnesses to the affect that Christ has in and on the world. Matthew also makes us witnesses to the *effects* of Christ—what emerges in us, what comes to fruition, owing both to our relationship with Christ and our sustained interaction with Matthew's Gospel. Matthew not only shows us what Christ brought to fruition and fulfillment *then*, but Matthew also shows us what Christ brings to fruition and fulfillment *now*.

Matthew accomplishes this by giving us insight into the multiple, complementary roles and identities that Jesus embodied and fulfilled. Matthew shows us Jesus as the Messiah, the Son of David, the Son of God, the Son of Man, the Great Teacher, and the Suffering Servant. Moreover,

Matthew portrays Jesus fulfilling all of these differing roles simultaneously. To put it another way, all of these roles come together in the concrete life of Jesus.

The complexity of Matthew's focus involves both personal responsibility and social action. He shows us, for example, the personal effects of Jesus's teaching in the Sermon on the Mount, as well as the social effects in the parables. Matthew also shows us ways in which the power of God operates in and through our willingness to assume responsibility in our interaction with others. He makes us witnesses to the presence of this unfolding power, which lies, as it were, just beneath the surfaces of the world in which we currently live (as in the painting by Richter). Perhaps most important to Matthew's purposes and designs, he makes us witnesses not only to the presence of the power by which God raised Jesus from the dead, but also to how that power brings righteousness to fulfillment in the concrete lives we live together.

The delightful challenge that Matthew's Gospel poses is that these insights can't be broken down into fragments. Matthew's Gospel isn't like a text message. It's more like a painting by Kay Hakoda or Gerhard Richter. The Gospel of Matthew isn't a mere sum of the parts. It is a mysterious whole. It is something for us to understand, to be sure. But (perhaps) more importantly, it is something for us to live with, to pay attention to, to feel, and to experience its effects in and through us. To put it another way, Matthew's Gospel is something to be treasured. Like Mark who went before him, Matthew seeks to open our eyes to the complex goodness, truth, and beauty of Jesus Christ—there and then, as well as here and now.

In writing this amazing Gospel, Matthew sought to bring about a transformation in the lives of his readers. Nothing would thrill me more than that you, dear reader, might enjoy the kind of transformation that Matthew hoped for in writing. To this end, in writing this little book, I hope to help you enjoy Matthew's complexity. Again, this isn't complicated, but it *is* more complex than text messaging. Like with music, it involves hearing the melody and discovering where it takes us. And like with a painting, it involves seeing the whole work at one time. As with other loves, it takes some effort, but the rewards are beyond calculation.

Matthew's goal is that both we and the world we live in might become both whole and new. That in itself makes reading Matthew with open eyes and hearts well worth our time and effort.

For Reflection

What is my experience with communication that is fragmented, versus communication that is successful? In my life, what makes for successful communication?

_____

_____

_____

What is my experience with wanting things to be simple, only to learn that they are more complex than I wish?

_____

_____

_____

What is my relationship with friendship, mystery, and beauty? How have I seen friendship grow with time (or deteriorate)?

_____

_____

_____

What kinds of presuppositions do I bring to the Bible? What do my presuppositions imply?

_____

_____

_____

What is my experience with sensing the presence of unseen reality that, although invisible, is nonetheless present and embodied in the life I live?

_____

_____

_____

What kinds of realities are emerging in my life and my relationships? What kinds of steps can I begin to take to bring these realities to fruition?

_____

_____

_____

What kinds of ideas about Christ do I hold? What is the significance of these ideas?

_____

_____

_____

What roles do personal and social responsibilities play in my faith? How are they similar and different?

_____

_____

_____

How have I witnessed fragmentation and wholeness in my life and relationships? What are the causes of fragmentation? What makes relationships whole?

_____

_____

_____

Chapter 2
beginning at the end
—the genesis of justice

In the Ancient Greek philosophy, the word form *meant, in the first instance, an inner forming activity which is the cause of the growth of things, and of the development and differentiation of their various essential forms. For example, in the case of an oak tree, what is indicated by the term 'formal cause' is the whole inner movement of sap, cell growth, articulation of branches, leaves, etc., which is characteristic of that kind of tree and different from that taking place in other kinds of trees. In more modern language, it would be better to describe this as* formative cause, *to emphasize that what is involved is not a mere form imposed from without, but rather* an ordered and structured inner movement that is essential to what things are. *Any such formative cause must evidently have an end or product which is at least implicit. Thus, it is not possible to refer to the inner movement from the acorn giving rise to an oak tree, without simultaneously referring to the oak tree that is going to result from this movement. So formative cause always implies final cause.*

—DAVID BOHM, *Wholeness and the Implicate Order*

Let it be so for now; for it is proper for us in this way to fulfill all righteousness.

—JESUS, in Matthew 3:15 (*NRSV*)

11

*W*hat are your conclusions about the Gospel of Matthew?"

This was the question that the woman put to me. It was my first meal at St. Deiniol's Library in Wales. I had arrived earlier that day after an overnight flight from the States. Although I had taken a nap, I was still groggy. I don't function well on too little sleep. As we sat down to dinner in St. Deiniol's newly refurbished dining room, I introduced myself to others at the table. The woman sitting next to me asked what I was working on. When I told her that I was writing on the Gospel of Matthew, it was then that she asked about my conclusions.

To respond to her question, I had to drag my mind from its yearning for hibernation. I was tired. I looked forward to being awake and engaged. But I wasn't there yet. My plan was to eat lightly and to go to bed and sleep—long and peacefully.

The woman apparently noticed my struggle to find an answer. She was afraid that she had asked a question that I could not answer. "Perhaps you intend to discover your conclusions while you are writing." This was a reasonable assumption on her part. One of the beauties of writing is that it so engages the mind that the writer can make discoveries as a part of the writing process. There are wonderful times when ideas surface as the essay unfolds. A mind fully engaged in writing becomes a magnet for ideas. Insights assimilate as the writer writes. This is certainly my experience. It is also the experience of many who find nourishment, if not sustenance, in writing as a hobby. Ideas emerge from within the writing process. No doubt, it was the experience of the woman who began our dinner conversation with a question about my conclusions.

The problem wasn't that I had not arrived at conclusions. I was simply tired. My mind hadn't planned on engaging Matthew until the next day. Matthew may have hungered and thirsted for righteousness, but on that evening, I hungered and thirsted for a good night's sleep. And yet, I wanted to give her a respectful answer, and I wanted the answer to be concise and clear. I have long held the view that one of the measures of the mastery of the material lies in one's ability to state an idea clearly. I don't mean that all ideas are simple. Many ideas are complex. To understand them takes time. Other ideas can be stated with simplicity. Because many simple ideas allow us to understand more complex ideas, the simple idea often requires unpacking, especially when the idea involves insight. The wonder of insight is that it makes it possible for us to see—to take in, to experience, and to understand more and more reality.

One of the wonders of Matthew as a Gospel writer is his stunning insight. There were matters about Christ that Matthew alone recognized. Mark, Luke, and John had their own insights, which we have every reason to believe are of equal importance. The joy of engaging the *four* Gospels is that each writer discovered insights into the life, death, and resurrection of Jesus Christ that are unique to the writer's particular Gospel. Each had spent substantial time reflecting on the continuing implications and consequences of the life of Christ. Their different insights don't place them in competition with each other. Instead, they complement each other. My students will occasionally ask me how it is that different writers might have different insights into the life of Christ. To illustrate, I point out to them that they know me primarily as teacher. My wife Nancy knows me as husband, our children Jaime and Dave know me as father, our daughter-in-law Chynnene knows me as father-in-law, and others know me as friend. Each has different insights into one person. This is what we get from the four Gospel writers: their insights into the lasting effects of the life of Christ.

This is what I wanted to convey to the woman who asked about my conclusions. Forcing open the door to the archives of memory, I found the answer she sought: *Matthew's insight was that the same power by which God raised Christ from the dead brings righteousness to fulfillment in the human heart. Matthew also recognized that righteousness comes to fulfillment through education. Righteousness is the fruit of teaching, learning, and living what we learn. To put it another way, Matthew recognized that the birth, life, death, and resurrection of Christ brought righteousness to completion. The means to righteousness is transformation through education—teaching and learning.*

The woman responded, "That makes sense." The dinner conversation then went off in another direction.

It was over a decade ago that I came to the realization that one of Matthew's foundational insights was that Christ brings righteousness to fulfillment in the human heart. I was taking a class at Wadham College at Oxford University. Our lecturer was the Scottish theologian, John Macquarrie. He had suggested that when we read the Gospels, we might pay attention to the first words that Jesus speaks. In making this suggestion, Macquarrie asked, "Wouldn't we expect that a Gospel writer would choose his first quotation of Jesus with great care? Wouldn't he select words that convey the overall purpose of his Gospel?"

Macquarrie's suggestion so captivated me that at the end of his lecture, I rushed to my room and examined the first words of Jesus in each of the Gospels. In Matthew's Gospel, Jesus first speaks in the third chapter: "Let it be so for now; for it is proper for us in this way to *fulfill all righteousness*." Jesus speaks these words at his baptism. John the Baptist had appeared at the Jordan River, where he was preaching a baptism of repentance for the forgiveness of sins. When the Pharisees and Sadducees came to John for baptism, he did not compliment them on the lives they had been living: "You brood of vipers! Who warned you to flee from the wrath to come? Bear fruit worthy of repentance. Do not presume to say to yourselves, 'We have Abraham as our ancestor'; for I tell you, God is able from these stones to raise up children to Abraham. Even now the ax is lying at the root of the trees; every tree therefore that does not bear good fruit is cut down and thrown into the fire. I baptize you with water for repentance, but one who is more powerful than I is coming after me; I am not worthy to carry his sandals. He will baptize you with the Holy Spirit and fire. His winnowing fork is in his hand, and he will clear his threshing floor and will gather his wheat into the granary; but the chaff he will burn with unquenchable fire" (3:7–12).

Why would John the Baptist target Pharisees and Sadducees for criticism? And why would he take aim at their claim to be descendants of Abraham? Matthew prepares us to anticipate John's prophetic criticism at the beginning of his Gospel with his genealogy—*the begats!* I am sympathetic with people who regard the first seventeen verses of the Gospel of Matthew less as a treasure of information and more as a cure for insomnia. The genealogy is admittedly dry reading. But for the one who is willing to dig, the genealogy will yield at least a pearl or two.

The first thing to notice is that Matthew's genealogy doesn't take us back to Adam (as does Luke's genealogy), but to Abraham (remember: the Pharisees and Sadducees stake their claim to authority on their connection to Abraham!). The next thing we notice is that this genealogy traces descent through the fathers. In other words, this is a *patri*lineal genealogy. And yet, this patrilineal genealogy mentions five women—Tamar, Rahab, Ruth, Bathsheba, and Mary the mother of Jesus. The women are the ones who make this genealogy interesting. What do we know about them?

The first is Tamar. We read about her in the thirty-eighth chapter of Genesis. Tamar was the daughter-in-law of Judah, one of the sons of Jacob. Tamar's first husband, Er, died. When a woman lost her husband, her brother-in-law was obligated to marry her (a custom called the *levirate*). In keeping with this custom, Judah gave Tamar to his son Onan for marriage. Because Onan refused to impregnate Tamar (this, he was also obligated to do), God struck Onan dead. This left Judah's youngest son, Shelah, to fulfill the obligations of marriage. Fearing for the life of this son, Judah withheld Shelah from Tamar. By doing so, Judah refused to render to Tamar her due.

When Tamar recognized the hopelessness of her circumstances, she removed her mourning clothes and dressed as a temple prostitute, which included wearing a veil. Tamar then offered herself to her father-in-law Judah. Because Judah did not recognize that the woman was his daughter-in-law, he unwittingly had sexual relations with her. At the time of their encounter, Judah could not offer payment to Tamar, but he did allow her to keep his signet ring and staff as collateral.

Tamar became pregnant, and her father-in-law was the father of her child. When Judah learned of Tamar's pregnancy, he ordered her execution. Tamar responded by sending Judah his signet ring and staff, along with a message: "The man to whom these belong is the man who impregnated me." Judah had the humility to confess, "She is more righteous than I." Judah's truthful response conveys a telling paradox: Tamar was a righteous prostitute. She was righteous in spite of Judah's failure of courage and his denying her customary justice.

Judah was the great-grandson of Abraham whom Matthew names in his genealogy. He identifies Judah in connection with his refusal to offer justice to his righteous daughter-in-law.

The next woman whom Matthew names is Rahab. So far as we know, she is the prostitute who assists Joshua and his Israelite army in the sack of Jericho. Because of her help, like Tamar, she, too, is a righteous prostitute. Because Rahab was also a Gentile—that is, a foreigner, one who cannot claim Abraham as ancestor—we might call her a righteous Gentile as well.

The same is true for the third woman whom Matthew names—Ruth. She, too, is a righteous Gentile. A Moabite woman, Ruth is completely loyal to her Israelite mother-in-law Naomi. And because Ruth proves her faithfulness to the Israelite, Boaz, he eventually marries Ruth, cementing this righteous Gentile's relationship to Israel.

The fourth woman whom Matthew cites is Bathsheba. Matthew refers to her not by name, but as "the wife of Uriah." By calling our attention to her in this way, Matthew first reminds us that David, the king of Israel, ordered the death of Uriah. When we then ask why David did so, we remember that while Uriah, a Gentile and a loyal soldier in David's army, was fighting on his king's behalf, David saw Uriah's wife as she was bathing, inquired as to her identity, sent for her, and had sex with her. Bathsheba became pregnant. And because Uriah refused to have sex with his wife during wartime (Uriah did not think it fair that he should have conjugal privileges that were denied to fellow soldiers), David ordered that Uriah be placed in the most vulnerable of positions on the battlefield. There, Uriah was killed by the enemy. Both Bathsheba and Uriah were the victims of David's ruthless concern for self alone. In that sense, both Bathsheba and Uriah were righteous: Uriah was a righteous Gentile, and Bathsheba, a righteous adulteress.

Why did Matthew name these four women in an otherwise patrilineal genealogy? Why did he find these particular women to be so significant? Each calls attention to the issue of righteousness—righteousness that is denied to some of the most significant women in Israel's story, or righteousness that these women, against overwhelming adversity, embody. Matthew's genealogy calls stark attention to the importance of justice and righteousness, including justice that is denied because of the failure of important leaders to implement justice owed to others.

Matthew wants us to embrace the significance of justice and righteousness for the descendants of all who aspire to the faith of Abraham. God called upon Israel to serve as a light of righteousness so that the world could witness righteousness in all its glory. Matthew also recognized that the implementation of justice and righteousness is rarely easy: "Enter through the narrow gate; for the gate is wide and the road is easy that leads to destruction, and there are many who take it. For the gate is narrow and the road is hard that leads to life, and there are few who find it" (Matthew 7:13–14). Moreover, there have been numerous times, marked by conspicuous occasions, when the people of God have failed to implement justice. Matthew recognized that this is so because taking the right path—the path of implementing justice—was not a consistent practice. Righteousness has not, to a sufficient degree, found abiding hospitality in the human heart. This is what we see in the stories of the four women, especially the stories of Tamar and Bathsheba. Judah and David were not possessed by sentiments of righteousness. Securing justice for others was not a matter of habit.

The final three figures in Matthew's genealogy are Joseph, Mary, and Jesus. They embody a new genesis—a new beginning—of justice and righteousness. Matthew understood Mary, Joseph, and Jesus to stand at the beginning of the final epoch in the genealogy of righteousness for the people of God. Mary is the final woman. And the birth of Jesus completes an otherwise incomplete lineage. Matthew's way of conveying this idea is ingenious. He points out that there are fourteen generations from Abraham to David, fourteen generations from David to the Babylonian exile, and fourteen from the exile to the birth of Jesus the Messiah. The number fourteen is a double seven, and seven is the number associated with creation: God created in six days and rested on the seventh. In the genealogy, with three groupings of fourteen, we have six sevens. Seven sevens will signal completion. Joseph, Mary, and Jesus stand at the beginning of the seventh seven: Through them, God inaugurates the fulfillment of righteousness.

We see this in Matthew's characterization of Joseph. Mary is Joseph's *betrothed* wife. Betrothal was somewhat like engagement for marriage in our culture, with this difference: a betrothed man and woman were legally married, but did not consummate their marriage for a period of one year.

Mary and Joseph were legally husband and wife, but they had not yet been physically intimate. And yet, Mary conceived a child from the Holy Spirit.

Joseph did not initially understand the cause of Mary's pregnancy. Nevertheless, Joseph was unwilling to subject Mary to public disgrace. From Joseph's initial viewpoint, Mary would have committed adultery. Adultery was a capital crime. For Joseph to save Mary from humiliation was also for him to save her life. Matthew gives the reason for Joseph's magnanimity: Joseph was a *righteous* man. Matthew not only characterizes Joseph in this way, but he also shows us Joseph in the act of *implementing* justice—of taking the right path, treating Mary in a just manner.

As Joseph resolved to divorce Mary without causing her harm, an angel of the Lord appeared to Joseph in a dream: "Joseph, son of David, do not be afraid to take Mary as your wife, for the child conceived in her is from the Holy Spirit. She will bear a son, and you are to name him Jesus, for he will save his people from their sins."

Joseph's obedience is nothing short of remarkable: He follows the instructions of the angel. He takes the right path, without counting the cost: By continuing in his marriage, Joseph himself would have suffered as the object of gossip and ridicule. People observing Mary with child would have presumed that Joseph violated the betrothal covenant by knowing his wife sexually before their marriage was complete. Joseph fulfilled righteousness by securing justice for Mary. But he did so at a potential cost to his own reputation. Joseph not only stood to lose face; he was vulnerable to total disgrace. Taking the right path and fulfilling justice would have been anything but easy. It was, however, a matter of incalculable importance.

Through Joseph and Mary, Matthew brought his remarkable genealogy to completion. Their purpose, their calling, was to give birth to the fulfillment of righteousness. This is more than sufficient to enable us to understand the significance of Jesus's first words—the ones he spoke at his baptism to John the Baptist. When Jesus presented himself for baptism, John objected: "I should be baptized by you!" Some scholars have suggested that Matthew was embarrassed by the idea of Jesus being baptized. Matthew's embarrassment is the reason they give for Jesus's intriguing response: "Let it be so for now; for it is proper for us in this way to *fulfill all righteousness.*" It does not appear to me that Matthew was embarrassed by Jesus's baptism. Instead, it appears that Matthew understood what Jesus understood: *righteousness is something that we embody and implement.* It isn't a mere idea; it is something we act on. It is in and through our just actions that righteousness comes to fulfillment. For Matthew, righteousness clearly involves our sentiments—the habits of our hearts. But it also involves the will—taking the right path. Righteousness has to do with taking into consideration the just interests of others and then doing what it takes to bring that justice to fulfillment. Fulfilling justice requires understanding, reflection, sentiment, and action that is both courageous and humble.

The word that Matthew used for justice is *dikaios. Dikaios* is one of those words that are polysemous: It has more than one meaning. *Dikaios* means *both* justice *and* righteousness. Moreover, in Matthew's way of thinking, justice and righteousness are inseparable. Perhaps the most important thing that Matthew wants us to see is that righteousness was not something that Jesus stood above or apart from. It was something that he embodied—in both heart (sentiments and understanding) and action (taking the right path, securing justice for others). Jesus's embodiment of righteousness stands at the heart of salvation from sin.

The first words that Jesus speaks in Matthew's Gospel are connected to the words that the angel speaks to Joseph: "She will bear a son, and you are to name him Jesus, for *he will save people from their sins.*" This is why it is important that Joseph seize upon the courage to take the right path: to implement justice for Mary. The birth of Jesus is for the purpose of saving people from their sin. As Jesus will show us in the Sermon on the Mount, sin involves a betrayal of our humanity through our militant unwillingness to take the right path and implement justice. One of Matthew's insights into the nature of sin is that it involves the obstinate refusal to do right for others. Righteousness transforms the human heart—particularly as we secure justice for others. This is true for Jesus. This is also true for Mary and Joseph.

I wish we could know the name of the artist. It is the one painting in the Louvre in Paris that stirs me the most. The painting hangs in Room 9. It is entitled *The Nativity*. Instead of listing the name of the artist, the placard simply reads, "Anonymous, France (1551)." The setting for the birth of Christ is a cathedral that is in ruins. The cathedral is at once both dark and luminous. At the same time, it is sufficiently solid that it can be rebuilt. The baby Jesus is being welcomed by little angels who, in unrestrained joy, are flying in and through the ruins of the cathedral. Every figure in this painting is smiling with complete happiness. They express the kind of glee of a child at the carnival— direct and utterly authentic.

What struck me as the most remarkable feature in this joyful painting is Joseph: He is the happiest of all. His hands, chest high and open to the baby Jesus, convey sheer astonishment coupled with gladness. Everything has come out just as the angel of the Lord told him it would. The results are perfect, and no one knows this better than he!

It is also clear in this *Nativity* that the cathedral in which the baby Jesus has been laid has long ago been abandoned. It is no longer a place that is used for official purposes. In ruins, and perhaps by neglect, this place has been, as it were, de-sanctified.

And yet, because of the presence of this particular baby, the cathedral of ruins is teeming with joy. Everyone is at play. The little angels are flying everywhere, like children thrilled to be on a roller coaster. One of them is racing down the stairs (has he forgotten that he can fly?) to report to Joseph and Mary that the cathedral has been deserted: *The place is empty! It's all ours!*

On the left is an ancient Roman bridge that leads to the ruins of the cathedral. The path is there. The foundation is still solid. The place is completely accessible. It needs simply to be visited and treasured.

Why is everyone so happy? The birth of *this* baby is the genesis of justice and righteousness. Mary, Joseph, and the baby Jesus are positioned at the climax of the Genealogy of Justice. This birth is the beginning of the fulfillment of righteousness. Everything in the genealogy will take a new path. Lives and cathedrals that are in ruins are in for big change!

For Reflection

How would I describe the form, or inner movement of my soul?

_____

_____

_____

In my life and relationships, where have I seen the fulfillment of righteousness? Where has righteousness yet to be fulfilled? What will it take for righteousness to come to fruition?

_____

_____

_____

In what sense is righteousness the fruit of learning and education? What will it take for education to prove fruitful?

_____

_____

_____

Matthew portrays four women—Tamar, Rahab, Ruth, and Bathsheba—as embodying righteousness. Why is this both surprising and important?

_____

_____

_____

What is the relationship between sentiments of righteousness and implementing righteousness? Are both important? Why, or why not? How are justice and righteousness related? Is it possible to have one without the other? Why, or why not?

_____

_____

_____

What is the significance of Joseph's righteousness? What did righteousness cost him? Had Joseph refused to implement righteousness, what might the cost have been?

_____

_____

_____

Why are justice and righteousness important in salvation from sin?

_____

_____

_____

In the renaissance painting, *Nativity*, what is the significance of the Christ-child being placed in cathedral ruins?

_____

_____

_____

Chapter 3

new from the old

Here, one has to emphasize that the act of reason is essentially a kind of perception through the mind, similar in certain ways to artistic perception, and not merely the associative repetition of reasons that are already known. Thus, one may be puzzled by a wide range of factors, things that do not fit together, until suddenly there is a flash of understanding, and therefore one sees how all these factors are related as aspects of one totality.

—DAVID BOHM, *Wholeness and the Implicate Order*

Therefore every scribe who has been trained for the kingdom of heaven is like the master of a household who brings out of his treasure what is new and what is old.

—JESUS, in Matthew 13:52 (*NRSV*)

The Gospels are so rich that every time I return to them, I see something that I had not noticed before. There is a simple reason for this: Matthew, Mark, Luke, and John are packed with meaning and insight—so much so that it isn't possible to be mindful of everything at once. The Gospels stand at the intersection of heaven and earth, past and present, old and new, time and eternity. They do so in the concrete here and how. For years, I have been fascinated by the question, what did biblical writers understand, and how did they come to their understanding?

It seems to me that both Matthew and Luke possessed a profound understanding of Mark, and that both used Mark as primary sources of meaning. Mark's insights into the life, death, and resurrection of Jesus are nothing short of astonishing. I also have the compelling impression that Matthew and Luke not only embraced Mark's insights, but also built on them, coming to astounding insights of their own. Matthew and Luke in turn composed their unique insights into their own Gospels.

When my students study the four Gospels, many are initially bothered by some of the differences that they see when taking a close look at what Matthew, Mark, Luke, and John have actually written. For understandable reasons, they tend to approach the Gospels under the assumption that the authors were mere reporters—literary video photographers who described what happened. One class period was particularly memorable. We read the accounts of Jesus's resurrection in each of the four Gospels. I let them make their own observations because I wanted to show them that there is much to be gained simply by paying close attention to what each writer actually wrote.

Their initial reading of the resurrection stories left them a bit perplexed. On the one hand, they were pleased that there was much for them to notice on their own—with little help from me. On the other hand, they were clearly seeing differences. This is what they saw: In Matthew's resurrection story, there is one angel, who is sitting on a stone outside of Jesus's tomb. In Mark, there is not an angel, but a young man inside the tomb. In Luke, there are two men inside the tomb. And in John, there are two angels inside the tomb. Turning to the details about the women, they noticed that in Matthew there are two women at the tomb; in Mark there are three; in Luke there are three named women, plus others who are not named; and in John, there is one woman. In Matthew, there is an earthquake (which does not happen in Mark, Luke, and John). And in John's Gospel, Peter and John race to the tomb (which does not happen in the other three).

When my students make these observations, they usually express eagerness to know what I think. The first thing that I tell them is that I do not make these observations because I am interested in discrediting the Gospels. What I *am* interested in is learning about each Gospel writer's uniqueness. Students usually seem surprised by this. Why would I take interest in a Gospel's uniqueness? Wouldn't I be more interested in what they report? Someone will usually bring up the idea of multiple witnesses to something like a car wreck: Each sees things differently. And yet, this same person will then put forth the idea of the inerrancy of scripture, which leads me to respond, "Wait a minute, how does the idea of the inerrancy of scripture square with the idea of multiple witnesses who see the same things, but report them differently? If the scriptures are inerrant in the manner that you suggest, wouldn't their observations all agree?"

In leading this discussion, I try to function as my students' ally as they explore the Gospels and ask questions. I want to express respect for them as believers, their reverence for the Bible, and the traditions from which they come. I wish that this had always been my approach to teaching. Alas, I am ashamed to say that in my younger and more arrogant days, I would have taken a measure of delight in blowing their doors off and proving them wrong. By the grace of God, I am no longer interested in Nietzsche's *philosophy with a hammer*. I now find the insights of the four Gospels merit anything but discrediting inasmuch as it is self-evident that the Gospels are transformative: The Gospels prepare us to live our own concrete lives with love, peace, and integrity. And this particular Gospel prepares us to live in righteousness—together.

I try also to give my students clear, honest answers. This is easier aspired to than accomplished. Honest answers are sometimes simple, but they are oftentimes complex. I wish once again to emphasize that I do not mean complicated. Too many scholars will confuse the complex (and beautiful) with the complicated. I have witnessed many learned people present their ideas in the most complicated manner so as to make them convoluted. By doing this, they try to position themselves as superior to their students. I find this kind of intellectual arrogance to be self-aggrandizing, needlessly confusing, and definitely unhelpful.

Simplicity often lies behind, or within, complexity. And simplicity sometimes provides the lens through which we can see, embrace, and understand more complex issues. One of the most simple of observations is that the Gospel writers each had insights into the life, death, and resurrection of Jesus that are unique. Their uniqueness doesn't make them contradictory, but complementary. Taken together, they give us a richer, more complete picture and understanding of Christ.

So how did Matthew use the insights of Mark? Mark's insights were so far-reaching that Matthew could both understand and build on them. Mark embodied his insights in his story of Jesus's baptism (Mark 1:9–11). This baptism story is not only concise; it represents Mark's entire Gospel in miniature. In other words, it is a (somewhat) simple story around which Mark built a more complex picture of Christ. When Jesus presented himself for baptism, John the Baptist submerged Jesus in the Jordan River. As in the books of Genesis and Exodus, the water of Mark's Gospel embodies chaos—the primordial abyss prior to creation: In the beginning, darkness covered the deep, unfathomable waters. In the story of Noah, God used the chaotic waters as an instrument of death and destruction. God did the same with the waters in the story of the Exodus: they were the instrument by which God destroyed the Egyptian army.

These are the waters from which Jesus emerged at his baptism: the primordial abyss of chaos, destruction, and death. In other words, at his baptism, Jesus emerged from the embodiment of the chaotic primordial past. As he did so, something equally remarkable happened. The heavens split open, the spirit of God descended on Jesus like a dove, and the voice of God spoke to Jesus: "You are my Son, the Beloved; with you I am well pleased." Whereas the waters embodied the primordial, archetypal past, the splitting of the heavens brought forth the apocalyptic future. This mystery is at once both simple and complex: Mark's story of the baptism of Jesus embodies the entire Gospel. Just as Jesus is submerged in the abyss of the primordial waters, so will Jesus be crucified and buried in the tomb. And just as the heavens split open when Jesus emerges from the waters, with the Spirit's descending on Jesus, so will God split open the heavens and raise Jesus from the dead. In its simplicity, the baptism in Mark embodies the entire Gospel, which then unfolds in ever greater complexity. Mark makes this clear in the calling of his first disciples. Jesus calls four fishermen to follow him. Why fishermen? Because following Jesus involves the mystery of assisting Jesus in casting his net into the deep and drawing people from whatever abyss they are drowning in and placing them on sufficiently solid ground.

One of the writers whom I admire has shared an episode from his own education that conveys something of Mark's insights into what it means to draw someone from the abyss and to place them on solid ground. His name is Robert Coles. Dr. Coles is a writer who has greatly expanded whatever capacity I have for understanding the four Gospels. Coles was a pediatric psychiatrist at Harvard. One of the things that made Coles effective as a practicing physician was his humility. If psychiatry was his day job, in the evenings Coles was an avid reader of the humanities. One of the consequences of this rich pursuit was that Robert Coles was not put off by mystery. Like Flannery O'Connor, whom Coles greatly admires, he knew that our lives are finally mysterious. Embracing mystery lay at the heart of both his humanity and his effectiveness as physician.

Robert Coles always recognized that he had a lot to learn. Some of his most important teachers were his patients. One was a young girl with leukemia. Today, medical science is able to help seventy to eighty percent of children who suffer with this frightening disease. Coles met this girl in the 1950s. At that time, the mortality rate from leukemia was high.

When Robert Coles visited the girl, she told him that she had been to the Red Sea.

"You have been to the Middle East?" he asked her.

"No. But I have been to the Red Sea."

"I don't understand. You say you've been to the Red Sea, but you've never been to the Middle East. What do you mean?"

The girl knew that Robert Coles liked children's drawings. Coles collected them, and one of the reasons was that the drawings helped him to *understand* children. She asked, "Would you like for me to draw you a picture?" Coles rounded up crayons and paper. He watched respectfully as she composed her drawing.

The girl first picked up a red crayon and then set it back down and selected a blue crayon. Coles watched her color in the bottom of the paper and thought, "This must be the ocean." She again picked up the red crayon, but returned to the blue and drew the sky. After that, she took a black crayon and was outlining clouds. She next picked up a yellow and drew the sun. Coles noticed that the sun, which was above the clouds, could not shine directly on the water. She then took a brown crayon and drew an island, on which she then drew green trees. It reminded Robert Coles of *Gilligan's Island*. She picked up a yellow, put it back down, and took an orange crayon and drew a human form on the sea. Then she picked up the red crayon and coated the blue water with red. Coles thought, "Aha, this is the Red Sea." Finally, the girl took a black crayon and drew an arrow from the human figure to the island.

"Here it is," the girl told Coles. "This is the Red Sea."

"What's this?" he asked.

"That's an island. If I get to the island, I'll be better."

"Then that's you on the Red Sea."

"Yes. Sometimes I don't think I'm going to make it."

Coles said, "I still don't understand. You said you've never been to the Middle East, yet you've been to the Red Sea."

Without speaking, she pointed at the bottle filled with blood. It was her transfusion. Robert Coles thought, "Of course. She has been floating in a sea of blood. This is what has been keeping her alive."

I am still moved by this story. Who cannot help but to be touched deeply by what this child conveyed—her vulnerability, the precariousness of her connection with the mystery of life, which we know to be a treasure. Like with Mark's story of Jesus's baptism, this girl knew herself to be drowning in her own Red Sea, from which she needed to be delivered. Moreover, she recognized that the sun (the heavens) was concealed by a cloud. She longed for the cloud to split open, for the sun to shine through, and to be delivered from the heartbreaking terror of her ominous personal abyss to the rock solid ground of the island.

These are the kinds of insights that Mark's Gospel conveyed. These are also the very insights that Matthew not only understood, but embraced. Moreover, Matthew took these astonishing insights and built on them. Matthew didn't contradict Mark; Matthew built on Mark. Matthew embraced Mark, but he also showed us mysteries that Mark's Gospel led to. If Mark focused more on the mystery of the terrifying abyss from which Christ delivers us, *Matthew gives us more insight into the nature of the solid ground on which Christ seeks to place us.* Like Mark, Matthew recognized that the power by which God created the heavens and the earth and raised Jesus from the dead also delivers us from whatever fearful abyss has swallowed us up and places us on solid ground. And like Mark, Matthew also understood that the power by which God raised Jesus from the dead bears the mystery of transformation. This mystery of transformation unfolds in Mark's Gospel in three more or less equal phases. The first phase involves a period of *recognition*, where we acknowledge and embrace reality as it is. The second phase involves *interpretation and reflection* on our circumstances as those very circumstances encounter the mystery of the power of God in which Christ stood, moved, and interacted with others. The third and final phase involves taking responsibility for *embracing, embodying, and implementing* the mystery of the presence of the power of God in those circumstances right where we are.

To summarize, the mystery of transformation that unfolds in Mark involves recognition, reflection, and implementation. These are the phases and movements of transformation that Matthew built on. But Matthew also knew that the time had come to explore more fully the mystery of the concrete, solid ground on which Christ places us. Whereas Mark explores the abyss, Matthew shows us the solid ground. Matthew recognized that *righteousness involves having a solid place on which to stand.* In other words, righteousness is one of the effects of the power of God that is involved in our concrete lives and circumstances. The same power by which God raised Christ from the dead brings righteousness and justice to fulfillment *in our world.* More than any of the other three Gospel writers, Matthew understood and conveyed the mystery by which the power of God gives birth to righteousness and brings it to fulfillment.

In Matthew's Gospel, it is to a life of justice and righteousness that Christ calls us. He urges us to join him in implementing righteousness by taking the narrow path of justice. He makes this especially clear near the end of the Sermon on the Mount (which is itself a solid place on which to stand!): "Enter through the narrow gate; for the gate is wide and the road is easy that leads to destruction, and there are many who take it. For the gate is narrow and the road is hard that leads to life, and there are few who find it" (Matthew 7:13–14). Then, at the end of the Sermon, Jesus portrays the end result of the life of righteousness: "Everyone then who hears these words of mine and acts on them will be like a wise man who built his house on rock. The rain fell, the floods came, and the winds blew and beat on that house, but it did not fall, because it had been founded on rock" (Matthew 7:24–25).

One of the things that I find fascinating is to reflect on little things that happen in Matthew that are unique to his Gospel. It isn't that I like to ponder them in isolation (like a verse of Scripture taken out of context), but in relationship to the entire Gospel. Matthew gives us one such pearl at the end of the thirteenth chapter, where Jesus begins to teach primarily in parables: "Therefore every scribe who has been trained for the kingdom of heaven is like the master of a household who brings out of his treasure what is new and what is old." Here, Matthew seems to portray *himself* as a scribe who prepares us to live in the kingdom of heaven—the world of God's sovereignty. Matthew saw himself as the master of a household, the bearer of a treasure. From the treasure, he brought out both the old—Mark's Gospel, the story of Creation, God's deliverance of the people from slavery—and the new—Matthew's own astounding insight into the mystery of the power that works in us to bring about justice that is built on rock-solid righteousness.

For Reflection

What experience have I had with "drowning," or being "swallowed-up" by circumstances that were "suffocating?" What made those experiences chaotic? What kind of "solid ground" was I in need of, or looking for?

_____

_____

_____

What is my experience with recognition? How might I characterize my life, relationships, and the circumstances in which I currently live?

_____

_____

_____

Were I to reflect on my life and circumstances in light of Matthew's Gospel, what parts of the Gospel speak most directly and compellingly to my situation and the world around me? How might Matthew interpret the life that I am living?

_____

_____

_____

What would it take for me to find more solid ground on which to stand and to live? What kinds of steps are necessary?

_____

_____

_____

In what sense does my life consist of broken pieces or fragments? What would it take for me to draw those pieces into a mysterious whole? What steps am I willing to take?

_____

_____

_____

Chapter 4
mind the gap!

Content and process are not two separately existent things, but, rather, they are two aspects of views of one whole movement. Thus fragmentary content and fragmentary process have to come to an end together.

—DAVID BOHM, *Wholeness and the Implicate Order*

The kingdom of heaven is like treasure hidden in a field, which someone found and hid; then in his joy he goes and sells all that he has and buys that field.

—JESUS, in Matthew 13:44 (*NRSV*)

The voice is ominous. At least, it attempts to be so. It is also ubiquitous. It is always there. Its purpose is to provoke vigilance with an aim at avoiding danger. The danger isn't evil, but it could involve life and limb. The voice speaks three words and three words only: *Mind the gap!* Anyone who has spent time in London will immediately recognize where they have heard the voice: the London Underground.

The words are a warning. In some of the Underground stations, there will be a gap between the train and the platform. Typically, the gap is an inch or two at most. On the day before I wrote this essay, I was in the Embankment Underground

Station in London. This time, when I heard the announcement, "Mind the gap!" I gave close attention. The gap between the platform and the train was almost a foot. It paid to be careful when boarding the train. If I didn't watch my step, I could end up falling and even breaking a leg. Minding the gap was the prudent thing to do.

Mind the gap! I think of these words every time I read the first beatitude. The setting is the Sermon on the Mount. Matthew gives us the sermon in chapters 5–7. The Sermon begins with nine beatitudes, none of which is more puzzling than the first: *Blessed are the poor in spirit, for theirs is the kingdom of heaven.* This is my favorite beatitude to explore with my students for one simple reason: The exploration opens their eyes to the flow of mystery in both Matthew's Gospel and in our concrete world.

I like to begin by giving them a literary term—caesura. I don't remember any student's having already encountered this term. I always assure them that it's a simple word that conveys a simple idea. A caesura is a break in poetry—a poetic pause. It's that simple. I then write the first beatitude on the board and ask them a question, "In this beatitude, where is the caesura? I have never had a class of students that failed to give the correct answer: "It's after the comma; it's between *spirit* and *for*. Blessed are the poor in spirit [pause] for theirs is the kingdom of heaven." That pause is the caesura.

That leads to a more important question: What do you notice about the break? Why is it there? What does it tell you?

Some puzzled, but inquisitive student will say, "It's strange. Those two clauses (Yes, they always have the presence of mind correctly to call them clauses!) don't fit together." This is where I begin to get excited. "Yes! There isn't just a poetic break; there's a gap. The gap is between poverty of spirit on the one hand and inheriting the kingdom of heaven on the other. Doesn't it seem strange for Jesus to begin his sermon with a declaration that those who inherit the kingdom of heaven—the world of God's sovereignty—are those who are spiritually impoverished?"

Someone will then ask me to help them understand what I mean by spiritual poverty: "What does it mean to be poor in spirit?"

"Well, what comes to mind if I say to you, 'Blessed are those who are spiritually rich?'"

The students have no problem answering that question. Their answers include great figures like Mother Teresa, Pope John Paul II, Billy Graham, Martin Luther King Jr., Nelson Mandela, Gandhi, or Bishop Desmond Tutu.

I can then ask, "So, if these are the spiritually rich, who are the poor in spirit?"

They respond, "Those of us who don't measure up to their example?"

"In other words, those who are poor in spirit—spiritually impoverished— are those who are unlike, say, Mother Teresa."

"Yes, that's right."

"Okay. Now tell me what's strange about this beatitude."

One of the students says, "I would expect Jesus to say that the rich in spirit, or spiritual giants, are the ones who will inherit the kingdom of heaven. That's where the gap is. It's between those of us who know we are spiritually impoverished and the kingdom of God. So why does Jesus put it that way? Why would he say that the *spiritually poor* inherit the kingdom of heaven?"

Ah, that's the sixty-four dollar question. And it is but the beginning of our investigation.

If the first blessing is the most puzzling of the *beatitudes*, I think that the most curious of *parables* is the Treasure Hidden in the Field: "The kingdom of heaven is like treasure hidden in a field, which someone found and hid; then in his joy he goes and sells all that he has and buys that field" (Matthew 13:44). When I put this parable in front of my students, I don't first ask, where's the gap? I begin with a more general question: What do you *notice* about this parable? What is it about this parable that is strange, odd, puzzling, or intriguing? This can be a little more challenging for students for the simple reason that many think of a parable as having a straightforward message or meaning that is completely without ambiguity. So I will usually have to follow up with additional questions. "Whose field was this?" Jesus didn't say. "Who was the man searching for the treasure?" Jesus didn't say. "How did he find the treasure?" Silence. "Was he searching for it? Was it just sitting out there on top of the ground?" No one can imagine that the treasure was just sitting there in plain sight! "So it was likely underground. How, then, did the guy find it? Did he have to dig in the owner's field? If so, did he leave it looking like it was plagued by a family of giant gophers? Jesus says that the man, having found the treasure, hid it back in the field. Did the owner know about the treasure?" He must not have; otherwise, why would he sell the field with the treasure still in it? "Jesus said that the man sold everything that he had. How much was the man who found the treasure worth? And how much was the field worth? In other words, *what was its value?*"

Because the answers to these questions aren't readily apparent, some student, with impatient exasperation, will demand, "*Why doesn't Jesus just tell us?*" This is a fair question. It sets up the second, and (thankfully) last lesson in literary interpretation for the day—poetic effect. I ask, "Can anyone help us understand what we mean by the words, poetic effect?" I rarely get a response to *this* question. Fortunately, like with the word *caesura*, poetic effect is a simple, straightforward, and fruitful concept. When we are reading the Bible (or any great literature, for that matter), it's important to ask not only what something says or means, but also what it *does*. In other words, what do the words accomplish? What *result* do they aim to produce? What *impact* do they have on us? When we consider the words, "Mind the gap," for example, the effect that the words aim for is straightforward: to insure the safety of those boarding the train. Many of my students are athletes. This means that I can draw on the world of collegiate competition for an analogy. I turn to the subject of *trash talk* as an example of poetic effect. Lots of the athletes engage in it, and all of them know what it is. So I will say, "Let's take trash talk as an example. When an athlete uses trash talk, what result is the athlete looking for?" The answer is always, "To distract your opponent; to get into your opponent's head." I will then say, "In other words, trash talk has a certain purpose, or goal. That's poetic effect. You are looking for a particular effect, or result. Now, would you use trash talk with your professor?" No, sir. "And would you use trash talk with your mother when you are telling her your grades?" *No way!* That's when you grovel!

Our conclusion is clear: Poetic effect has to do with what the words *do*—what they accomplish, the result that they produce. In Matthew's case, poetic effect has to do with the sense of mystery that the Gospel brings forth in the human heart. Poetic effect is an important concept when it comes to understanding the Parable of the Treasure Hidden in the Field: The parable does something to us. But not once does Jesus simply tell us what it means. Instead, he lets the parable work its mystery and render its effect, which is to provoke curiosity and wonder. The parable breathes marvel into every nook and cranny of our consciousness. *What was the treasure? How did it get there? How did the man find it? Was he looking for it? Who was this man? Why doesn't Jesus tell us his name? What was the treasure worth? What was he worth?* The parable opens us to mystery, and that's not a bad place to be.

To complete our investigation on the Treasure, it's important to ask, where is the gap in this story? Because I don't want to lose my students or to leave them hanging, when asking them, *where is the gap*, I hasten to add that in this parable, the gap is not a caesura (like with the first beatitude). Instead, the gap is in the picture that the parable draws in the landscape of our imaginations. The gap is what we visualize when we hear this parable: The gap is in the field. In the Parable of the Treasure Hidden in the Field, the gap is in the earth. The gap is the hole in the field in which the treasure is hidden.

This is what we can't afford to miss: In the Gospel, Matthew bears witness to what he saw. By showing us what he saw, he teaches *us* how to see. Matthew shows us a gap—two for that matter. The first is in the beatitudes. There is a gap between poverty of spirit and inheriting the kingdom of heaven. This raises that all-important question, how is it that the spiritually impoverished inherit the kingdom of heaven? In other words, what fills the gap in our lives? Then, the Parable of the Treasure Hidden in the Field provides a clue: There is a gap in the earth, and in the gap is a hidden treasure. The treasure is beyond measure. Jesus doesn't place a price tag on it. Its value is beyond calculation. The treasure is priceless. Still, we don't yet know what the treasure is. But before moving on, it's important to pause and reflect: The nature and contents of the treasure are a mystery. At the same time, as we read the parable and reflect on the curiosity that the parable embodies, we can recognize that the Treasure Hidden in the Field comes to occupy our imaginations. At the same time, the treasure is not the property of our imaginations. We know about the treasure only because of this parable. The effect of the parable is to make us aware of the riches of a treasure that fills the gap of our own spiritual poverty. That treasure mystery—it is the property of the kingdom of heaven, but through the parable, it comes to fill the gap in our imaginations.

This brings us to the all-important question, what is the treasure? To unravel this mystery, we carry our investigation to the very end of the Gospel (chapters 27–28). This is where Jesus was crucified, buried, and raised from the dead. When helping my students unravel Matthew's mysteries, I call their attention to what is unique to Matthew's Gospel—characteristics which he alone attributes to the crucifixion and resurrection. I first quote from the climax of the crucifixion. Here, I place words that are distinctive to Matthew in italics. At the end of the crucifixion, "Jesus cried with a loud voice and breathed his last. At that moment the curtain of the temple was torn in two, from top to bottom. *The earth shook, and the rocks were split. The tombs also were opened, and many bodies of the saints who had fallen asleep were raised. After his resurrection they came out of the tombs and entered the holy city and appeared to many.* Now when the centurion and those with him, who were keeping watch over Jesus, *saw the earthquake and what took place*, they were terrified and said, "Truly this man was God's son" (27:50–54).

A few verses later, Jesus was buried: "Joseph took the body and wrapped it in a clean linen cloth and laid it in his own new tomb, *which he had hewn in the rock. He then rolled a great stone to the door of the tomb and went away.* Mary Magdalene and the other Mary were there, sitting opposite the tomb" (27:59–61).

Next, Matthew writes of the securing of the tomb. The chief priests and the Pharisees approached Pilate and asked him to set guards at the tomb in order to prevent Jesus's disciples from breaking into the tomb, taking his corpse, in order to claim (falsely) that Jesus was raised from the dead. Pilate told them that they could use their own soldiers. So the chief priests and Pharisees "went with the guard and *made the tomb secure by sealing the stone*" (27:66).

The final puzzle piece involves the resurrection itself. Matthew begins his narrative of the resurrection as follows: "After the Sabbath, as the first day of the week was dawning, Mary Magdalene and the other Mary went to see the tomb. *Suddenly there was a great earthquake; for an angel of the Lord, descending from heaven, came and rolled back the stone and sat on it.* His appearance was like lightning, and his clothing white as snow. For fear of him the guards shook and became like dead men. But the angel said to the women, "Do not be afraid; I know that you are looking for Jesus who was crucified. He is not here; for he has been raised, as he said. Come, see the place where he lay" (Matthew 28:1–6).

As with the Parable of the Treasure Hidden in the Field, Matthew has once again shown us the field of the earth—this time, the tombs of the saints who had died before Jesus, and the tomb of Jesus himself. In the stories of the crucifixion and resurrection, the gap in the earth is the tomb.

Here, then, is the important question: What happens when we synchronize the Beatitude, the Parable of the Treasure, and the Crucifixion and Resurrection? What is the treasure that is hidden in the tomb?

The treasure is Jesus and the power by which God raised Jesus from the dead. The resurrected Christ and the power by which God raised him from the dead are the treasure. By this same power, God also raised the bodies of the saints who had died. This power shakes the earth. The power by which God raised Jesus from the dead is not the property of the landscape itself (the earth, or the tombs in which Jesus and the saints have been buried) anymore than the treasure hidden in the field is the property of the landscape of the human soul. The treasure is not measureable. It is the property of God. The treasure is the mystery which God poured into the gap in the field of the earth and raised Jesus from the dead. This is the same mystery with which God fills the gap in the field (the soul) of the impoverished spirit. It is the birthright of those who want to follow Christ. It is the power that delivers us from the abyss of injustice and sin. This is the power that transforms us, giving birth to righteousness.

There are other clues that Matthew gives that facilitate our recognizing this mystery. At the end of the twelfth chapter, Jesus says that a tree is known by the fruit that it bears. The fruit of which he speaks consists of the results of the choices that we make: "How can you speak good things when you are evil? For out of the abundance of the heart the mouth speaks. The good person brings good things out of a good treasure, and the evil person brings evil things out of an evil treasure" (12:34–35). Here, fruit and treasure are at least in part synonymous. In the episode that immediately follows, the scribes and the Pharisees demand that Jesus show them a sign. Jesus's response alludes directly to his resurrection from the dead: "An evil and adulterous generation asks for a sign, but no sign will be given to it except the sign of the prophet Jonah. For just as Jonah was three days and three nights in the belly of the sea monster, so for three days and three nights the Son of Man will be in the heart of the earth" (12:39–40). Here, Matthew has brought the subjects of treasure, earth, and resurrection into close proximity with his allusion to Jonah. It is in the next chapter that Matthew gives us the Parable of the Treasure Hidden in the Field. Even though I did not see the connection between the gaps in the Beatitudes, the treasure hidden in the gap of the field, and the resurrection of Jesus from the dead until I finished the Gospel, Matthew actually prepares us to see this connection in what unfolds prior to the parables in chapter thirteen.

What Matthew uncovers is a synchronicity between the gap in the field of the human spirit and the poetic gap in the field of the earth. We can sense the gap in the recognition of our own poverty of spirit. At the same time, Matthew shows us this same gap in the other beatitudes: "Blessed are those who mourn, for they will be comforted" (Matthew 5:4). There is a gap between the soul in grief on the one hand and the joy of comfort on the other. "Blessed are the meek, for they will inherit the earth" (5:5). Who are the meek? Those who refuse to harm others? Perhaps. Those who suffer harm? Probably. What, then, does it mean to inherit the earth? For Matthew, the earth is his metaphor for justice and righteousness— the solid place on which to stand. Does the one who suffers harm feel solid ground underneath? Not usually. "Blessed are those who hunger and thirst for righteousness, for they will be filled" (5:6). The hunger for righteousness recognizes that we aren't there yet. There is a gap in the human soul: Righteousness is in short supply. Because of the gap, our world suffers from a scarcity of justice. When we embrace and grieve our spiritual poverty, then we can recognize harm we have either suffered or caused. We can recognize times that we neither embraced righteousness nor implemented justice. If this awareness of the gap in our souls becomes the hunger and thirst for righteousness, we open ourselves to the treasure hidden in the field—the power by which God raised Christ from the dead. This same power brings righteousness to fulfillment in the human heart.

As the Beatitudes continue, they show us a life engaged in the power of God: "Blessed are the merciful, for they will receive mercy. Blessed are the pure in heart, for they will see God. Blessed are the peacemakers, for they will be called children of God. Blessed are those who are persecuted for righteousness' sake, for theirs is the kingdom of heaven" (Matthew 5:7–11). When we actively offer mercy to others, we receive mercy because we implement the power of God. When we hunger for righteousness by embracing the power of God in the gap in our souls, we then recognize God right before our eyes (see Matthew 25:31—26:16, for example). And lest we confuse our own willingness to embrace and implement the power of God with our own (alleged) righteousness, Jesus ends the Beatitudes by clearing up any illusions of ease: "Blessed are you when people revile you and persecute you and utter all kinds of evil against you falsely on my account. Rejoice and be glad, for your reward is great in heaven, for in the same way they persecuted the prophets who were before you" (5:11–12). Jesus leaves no room for either boasting or playing the role of the victim. What he does instead is to open our eyes to the presence of the power of God and the rock of righteousness on which his power finally places us.

In the summer of 2008, I enjoyed the pleasure of seeing a painting in the National Gallery of Modern Art in Prague, Czech Republic. The artist is Maxim Kopf, who was born in 1892 in Víden and died in 1958 in Twin Farms, Vermont. The painting is entitled "The Vision" (1920). It features exactly what the title suggests: A man is receiving a vision from heaven. The man himself is in ecstasy. It is not surprising that he is completely enveloped in light. The source of the light, however, is ambiguous, raising the question, where does the light come from—above, or below? We might first be inclined to think that the light comes from above, but the beam of light, which is V-shaped, comes to a point in the earth, just below the feet of the visionary. If the source of the visionary light is from above the man, its origins are of great width and breadth, converging and coming to a point just beneath where he stands, or is lifted up from the earth. At the same time, Kopf portrays that the light could just as well be coming from beneath the visionary, with its source *in* the earth, bearing him up. If this is the effect that the artist sought, he has, wittingly or without conscious intent, allowed the viewer to witness what Matthew shows in the combination of the Treasure Hidden in the Field, the Crucifixion, and the Resurrection of Jesus from the Dead: a power that belongs to the kingdom of heaven, which either emerges from the earth, or converges beneath the surface of the earth. Either way, it is a visionary power that we, by the grace of Matthew's Gospel and Maxim Kopf's painting, can imagine. It is a treasure that is neither the property of the fields of the earth nor the landscape of the human spirit. The treasure belongs to God. At the same time, the treasure is unequivocally proper to the landscape of the human spirit. It fits the gap of human impoverishment just as the treasure fills the hole in the field. This same treasure, the power by which God raised Christ from the dead, is what brings righteousness to fulfillment in the human spirit and justice to fulfillment in our world.

The power by which God raised Christ from the dead is what transforms those of us who are spiritually impoverished, fitting us for the world of God's sovereignty. It is the same treasure that comforts those who mourn. It is the power by which those who seek not to damage or harm others come to inherit the earth. It satisfies people whose hunger and thirst are for righteousness. It is the power by which the merciful receive mercy. And because it is the power by which the poor in spirit are transformed, it is the power by which we become pure so as to recognize God at large in our world.

The reason that Matthew exhorts us to *mind the gap* is that the gap is where we will find the mystery of the power of God.

For Reflection

Who are the people in my life who are spiritually rich? What makes them so?

_____

_____

_____

Where, in my life, have I found myself spiritually depleted or impoverished?

_____

_____

_____

What is my experience with being open or closed to power and grace that is outside of myself?

_____

_____

_____

What kinds of things am I most curious about? What gives me a sense of wonder?

_____

_____

_____

Where does my sense of wonder and curiosity connect me to mystery and God?

_____

_____

_____

What would it take for me to synchronize the gap in my own life with the Treasure Hidden in the Field?

_____

_____

_____

What would it take for me to hunger and thirst for mercy and righteousness?

_____

_____

_____

What steps will I take to open myself to the power by which God raised Christ from the dead?

_____

_____

_____

How is openness to this power related to the ways in which I serve others?

_____

_____

_____

Chapter 5
the rock of righteousness

When we really grasp the truth of the one-ness of the think-ing process that we are carrying out, and the content of thought that is the product of this process, then such insight will enable us to observe, to look, to learn about the whole movement of thought and thus to discover an action rel-evant to this whole, that will end the 'turbulence' of move-ment which is the essence of fragmentation in every phase of life.

—DAVID BOHM, *Wholeness and the Implicate Order*

Blessed are you, Simon son of Jonah! For flesh and blood has not revealed this to you, but my father in heaven. And I tell you that you are Peter, and on this rock I will build my church, and the gates of Hades will not prevail against it.

—JESUS, in Matthew 16:17-18 (*NRSV*)

"Have you ever been to Iona?"

"No. Have you?"

"No, but I want to go there someday."

I asked her why. She told me that the island of Iona is one of those places where the veil that separates the spiritual and material worlds is thin.

That was all she needed to say. I was hooked. I was curious to know what it would be like to experience a place where it is self evident that the veil is thin. I also wanted to know what it all means. What is the significance of this kind of place? What kind of impact would it have on my soul? Would something emerge within me? Would it make a difference? Would it help me to grow? Would it transform me? Would it help me become a better person?

I first needed to learn something about the place. Iona is a tiny island— one mile by three miles. Its significance began with St. Columba. Fleeing Ireland in 563 A.D., Columba resolved to settle on the first island where he could no longer see Ireland. This was the island of Iona, just off the west coast of Scotland in the Hebrides. Columba, with twelve followers, built a monastic community on the island. From the island, they introduced Christianity to the people of Scotland. In the early ninth century, these Celtic monks produced the *Book of Kells* (an illuminated manuscript of the Gospels, which is now on display at Trinity College in Dublin). And in the early thirteenth century, a Benedictine Abby was built, which has been restored during the last one hundred years. Today, all are welcome to make a pilgrimage to the Abby and even participate in retreats with the Iona Community.

J. Philip Newell, the former Warden of the Abby, says that on Iona, it is possible to listen for the heartbeat of God. When I read this, I was completely intrigued. What could this possibly mean? One of the most transformative experiences of my life was the singular privilege of spending a week at the Abby on retreat. I went to the island with a question: How do you know when you are hearing the heartbeat of God? How do you *recognize* when the veil is thin? How do you know when you are seeing both the material and spiritual? What does it look like when the veil separating heaven and earth grows so thin that the heavens split open?

When I arrived at Iona, I received my room assignment in the Abby cloisters. After unpacking, I went into the Abby Church to pray. I was feeling excited. I approached Iona with a sense of childlike wonder and anticipation. But I also went with some anxiety. I was at Iona during a time in my life when I wanted to make changes in the way I was living. I wanted to become more centered, calm, stable, dependable, autonomous, deliberate, and when circumstances warranted, courageous. In Matthew's terms, I needed to become more steadfast—righteous and just. As I sat in the Abby Church for the first time, I kept hearing the words "Don't be afraid." I closed my eyes, and tried to give my undivided attention to God. The words "Don't be afraid" continued. As I calmed myself down, I listened for the Voice of God. What was I hearing in my imagination? And how would I know that what I was hearing was authentic? I wrote these words in my journal: "I am praying with you. Put away all anxiety. I am here now. I will be speaking to you all throughout the week. You will be hearing my Voice—in your imagination. Some of your thoughts will be from Me. I will patiently reiterate all that I have to say to you, that you might grow accustomed to my Voice, and that you may know and understand. Don't be anxious. I will be awakening you. Don't try to rush the process. I am the great Teacher. I am your Teacher. Don't be afraid." To this day, these words resonate with authenticity. They open a pathway to the confident and calm. This is the Voice of the Genuine.

Having recorded these words in my journal, I began to walk through the old stone Abby Church. As I did so, I felt an inclination—an inner prompting—to reach out and touch one of the great stone pillars that are the foundation of the Abby Church. I didn't know why. But as I did so, I continued to pray.

It was that evening, during the closing nine o'clock worship service, that I discovered why. The leader of the service was praying on behalf of the entire Iona Community. She was thanking God that "this stone church had served as protection for many who were poor, persecuted, and suffering." It was then that understanding began to emerge: *My inklings and this stone Abby Church are intimately connected.*

Following breakfast on the first morning, the Iona Community cleaned the Abby. I was assigned the job of vacuuming the common room. I learned that the British call this "Hoovering." After my chores, I went into the Abby Church, where there is a Quiet Corner—a place set aside for solitude and personal prayer. I sat there with my journal. As I prayed, I heard the Voice, speaking softly, with complete confidence and compassion: *Just as you swept the common room this morning, during this week, I will be sweeping the temple of your soul, cleansing your soul from sin. Just as my Son cleansed the Temple, so will I be cleansing you—forgiving your sin and sweeping the sin from your life.* As soon as I heard these words, I heard a sweeping sound. One of the members of the Iona Community was sweeping the floor of the Abby Church, in preparation for worship. As I heard her doing so, I knelt in front of the open book in the Quiet Corner and read the words, "Happy are the pure in heart; the kingdom of heaven is theirs. Happy are the gentle; the earth shall belong to them. I am the friend of those who know themselves to be impure of heart."

There it was. Christ is the friend of those who, knowing themselves to be impure, seek transformation. Christ is the Advocate. He was with me— right then and there in the Quiet Corner of the Abby Church—sweeping my soul, cleansing me from sin.

This was one of those rare periods of time during which I managed to be present. Because I wasn't detached from where I was, I wasn't in a panic, wanting to escape into a disembodied, unconnected future. Thankfully, being fully present, I was also becoming less tense. In my intuition, I was beginning to recognize what it means to say that the veil is thin: *When we lay aside all distractions and are fully present, we live at the intersection between time and place.* The veil is thin when we live right here, right now—in the present moment where we are. Another way to put it is this: God is at the intersection between time and place. Presence is a matter of eternity.

What most puzzled me when I was at Iona was the intuitive motivation to reach out and feel the pillar of the great stone Abby Church. What surprised me was to hear the worship leader: *This stone church had served as protection for many who were poor, persecuted, and suffering.* The Iona Community recognized a connection between the protection that the stone Abby Church offered and the beatitude, "Blessed are the pure in heart." Upon reflection, they had come to the intuitive recognition that Christ is the friend of those who know themselves to be impure of heart. There is a connection between the landscape of the human soul and the architecture of the Abby Church. Just as Christ cleansed the Temple, a member of the Iona Community swept the Abby Church. So also was I a partner in sweeping the floor of the common room. These gestures and actions embodied and reflected Christ's beginning to cleanse the landscape of my soul.

Being present in the stone church, along with reading words of the beatitude in the Quiet Corner also brought me into the presence of the Gospel of Matthew. Not only is Matthew the Gospel writer who explores how it is that the power of God that raised Christ from the dead brings righteousness to fulfillment, but Matthew also features the poetic element of earth, or rock: To use an element such as rock poetically simply means that the author uses earth and rock to convey the reality and experience of righteousness. This makes the experience concrete or real in the human imagination. Among the four elements of earth, fire, air, and water, earth or rock is particularly fitting for the portrayal and embodiment of righteousness. This is because *righteousness involves having a solid place on which to stand.* Matthew's Gospel embodies the rock of righteousness. The justice that the power of God brought to fulfillment in Christ is rock solid—stable and completely dependable. Absent righteousness, life devolves into an abyss of chaos, leaving us without bearings.

One of the things I love about poetry is that words have the capacity to carry more than one meaning. When John the Baptist confronted those who thought of themselves as righteous, his words were piercing: "Do not presume to say to yourselves, 'We have Abraham as our ancestor'; for I tell you, God is able *from these stones* to raise up children to Abraham" (Matthew 3:9). At first glance, the words "from these stones" suggest a kind of mysterious transformation. In C. S. Lewis's novel, *The Lion, the Witch, and the Wardrobe*, Aslan the Lion breathes on stone statues, and they are transformed back into the living creatures that they were before the White Witch turned them into stone. It isn't difficult to associate the image of Aslan with the image of God's raising children to Abraham from stones. At the same time, as we explore Matthew's Gospel, we discover that he uses stone—earth and rock—to express the solidity of righteousness. To begin, Matthew wanted us to be mindful that when God gave the Decalogue (Ten Commandments) to Moses, God called Moses to climb to the top of the mountain (earth), where God presented to Moses words written on *stone* tablets. For Matthew, righteousness is solid just as the rock of earth is solid as well.

What can we see by scanning the Gospel, paying close attention to Matthew's use of earth and rock? We see that following the baptism of Jesus, the Spirit led Jesus into the wilderness, where he faced the devil. Having fasted for forty days and nights, Jesus was famished. Confronting Jesus in his hunger, the devil challenged Jesus to "command these stones to become loaves of bread" (4:4). Jesus refused: "It is written, 'one does not live by bread alone, but by every word that comes from the mouth of God.'" The words of God are rock solid. When Moses climbed Mount Sinai to receive the word of God, The Ten Commandments, the words were written in stone. These are the words that engender righteousness. Satisfying hunger is of incalculable importance, as Matthew shows us later in his Gospel—especially when it comes to providing food for those who suffer with debilitating hunger. Matthew is showing us that when satisfying our own hungers and cravings takes priority over living a life of righteousness and securing justice for others, we compromise our own humanity and attack the dignity of others.

What, then, is Matthew conveying when showing us John the Baptist claiming that God could raise children of Abraham from stones? It is hard for me to imagine that he was talking about turning rocks into people, for this would resemble Jesus's turning stone into bread. I think, instead, that Matthew was suggesting that God raises children to Abraham by standing us squarely on the rock of justice and righteousness.

In the second temptation (Matthew 4:5–7), the devil confronted Jesus with the idea of jumping from the pinnacle of the temple. Such a dare-devil stunt would be spectacular, transforming Jesus into an instant celebrity, for in the ninety-first Psalm, it is written that God will give his son command of his angels, which will bear him up so that his son will not dash himself on stone and injure himself. What could be more impressive? The problem is that were Jesus to do so, he would be squandering righteousness for notoriety. But the personal effect for the effort to impress others, to be sensational, or to make a spectacle of self, would be like dashing our bodies on stone. In other words, in our efforts to appear dashing in the eyes of others, we in reality damage ourselves by clashing with the rock of righteousness. When we try to use God to promote our own celebrity, we are putting God to the test.

The willingness to put God to the test naturally leads to the third temptation—self worship (Matthew 4:8–11). The devil took Jesus to a high mountain and showed him all the kingdoms of the world, promising Jesus unilateral power over others if Jesus will but fall down and worship the devil. Confronted with this temptation, Jesus has the presence of mind to dismiss the devil. It is written that we shall worship God alone. Like Moses, Jesus will climb a mountain, but his motive won't be the domination of others. Jesus's purpose will be to help people understand the righteousness of God through the Sermon on the Mount.

In the previous essay on the "Genesis of Justice," we saw how Matthew shows us that the fulfillment of justice and righteousness lies at the heart of Matthew's penetrating insight into the life of Christ. By portraying the righteousness of Christ as rock, Matthew brings us to the heart of mystery: His Gospel embodies and conveys the power by which God places us squarely on the rock of righteousness and justice. Matthew saw that transformation by means of righteousness and justice lies at the heart of mystery—both Jesus's teaching in the Gospel and the power by which God raised Jesus from the dead. Matthew's Gospel makes it possible for us to recognize that righteousness and justice also characterize the landscape of the human spirit at its best. We are most fully human when righteousness and justice shape the landscape on which we live our lives and interact with each other. In saying this, I refer both to the landscape of the human spirit (personal righteousness) and righteousness implemented for the sake of others (justice, or social righteousness). For Matthew, the two cannot be separated. Personal righteousness and social justice come to fulfillment in unbroken wholeness—as we implement righteousness, we are transformed. This is why Matthew embodies the solidity of righteousness with poetic images of earth and rock. He wants to build an interior landscape of rock solid righteousness as we implement and secure justice for others. Matthew's Gospel facilitates the process as it fills our imaginations with images of the earth. Consequently, when Jesus gives his most extensive portrayal of the foundation of righteousness, he does so standing on the top of a mountain, which was the kind of place where God gave the teachings of the law to Moses. Matthew, in other words, gives us Jesus's Sermon *on the Mount*. At the climax of this sermon, Jesus completes his portrayal of righteousness by employing two compelling images. The first involves an exhortation: "Enter through the narrow gate; for the gate is wide and the road is easy that leads to destruction, and there are many who take it. For the gate is narrow and the road is hard that leads to life, and there are few who find it"

(7:13–14). Effecting justice through righteousness cannot happen when we habitually take the easy road. Righteousness does, however, involve walking squarely on the earth in the implementation of justice. Later in the Gospel, Jesus says, "Come to me, all you that are weary and are carrying heavy burdens, and I will give you rest. Take my yoke upon you, and learn from me; for I am gentle and humble in heart, and you will find rest for your souls. For *my yoke is easy, and my burden is light*" (11:28–30). Matthew's Gospel embodies a paradox: The easy yoke and light burden of Christ complement the difficult road of righteousness. And how does Christ lighten our load? By satisfying the hungers by which we are tempted to squander righteousness for our own satisfaction, by lifting the burden of our need for celebrity, and by removing from us the desire to sell our souls to the devil so that others will do our will.

Lightly yoked, we build on solid righteousness, as Jesus tells us at the conclusion of his sermon: "Everyone then who hears these words of mine and acts on them will be like a wise man who built his house on rock. The rain fell, the floods came, and the winds blew and beat on that house, but it did not fall *because it had been founded on rock*. And everyone who hears these words of mine and does not act on them will be like a foolish man who built his house on sand. The rain fell, and the floods came, and the winds blew and beat against that house, and it fell—and great was its fall!"

Like with the other three Gospels, one of the benefits of Matthew's Gospel is that he sharpens our focus. His insights into the life of Christ and the nature of the good news help us to embrace and to recognize mysteries that we might otherwise avoid. One of those mysteries is the story of Jesus's transfiguration (Matthew 17:1–13). As with Mark's transfiguration story, Matthew's follows one of the most important episodes in the Gospel, an episode from Mark that Matthew both embraces and expands. Jesus and his disciples were traveling to Caesarea Philippi, which is north of the Sea of Galilee. As they made their journey, Jesus was asking them what people have been saying about him: "Who do people say that the Son of Man is?" Jesus's disciples correctly answered that some identified him as John the Baptist, some Elijah, and others as Jeremiah or one of the other prophets. Jesus then asked his disciples who *they* thought Jesus was. Peter responded, "You are the Messiah, the Son of the living God."

In Mark's Gospel, Jesus responded to Peter by demanding his silence on the matter. Jesus didn't want Peter speaking about Jesus publicly. In Matthew, Jesus's immediate response to Peter was one of confirmation and celebration: "Blessed are you, Simon son of Jonah! For flesh and blood has not revealed this to you, but my Father in heaven. And I tell you, you are Peter [in Greek, *Petrós*], and on this rock [*Petrá*] I will build my church, and the gates of Hades will not prevail against it. I will give you the keys of the kingdom of heaven, and whatever you bind on earth will be bound in heaven, and whatever you loose on earth will be loosed in heaven" (Matthew 16:17–19). Matthew recognized that Christ calls the church to be a rock of righteousness, a people firmly set on justice.

Immediately after this exchange between Jesus and Peter, Matthew returned to the story just as Mark told it. Jesus did not want his disciples talking about him. It seems that because their understanding of Jesus was far from adequate, they were not yet qualified to teach. We see this in what follows: Jesus instructed his disciples about the necessity and importance of his suffering, death, and resurrection. Peter's reaction was to take Jesus aside and to rebuke him: "God forbid it, Lord! This must never happen to you" (Matthew 16:22). In response to Peter, Jesus words could not have been more devastating: "Get behind me, Satan!" Matthew then uniquely added, "You are a *stumbling block* to me; for you are setting your mind not on divine things but on human things" (16:23). What does Matthew show us? The church is called to be a solid foundation of righteousness—a body of people whose ongoing commitment is to bring justice to fulfillment, to make it a reality. For Peter to reject the possibility of Christ's suffering was for him to reject both the narrow door and the house founded on rock. Instead, Peter was opting for the path of ease, not yet realizing that this is the path that trips people up, leading ultimately to destruction.

It is at this point that Matthew's Gospel portrays another paradox that renders the path through the narrow door difficult: "If any want to become my followers, let them deny themselves and take up their cross and follow me. For those who want to save their life will lose it, and those who lose their life for my sake will find it. For what will it profit them if they gain the whole world but forfeit their life? Or what will they give in return for their life?" (16:24–26). A part of the paradox is that Christ claims that entering the narrow door and taking up the cross is Christ's easy yoke. The reason is that this road leads into the house built on the solid foundation.

It is at this point in the narrative that Matthew presents the story of The Transfiguration (in chapter 17). Matthew begins by telling us that after six days, Jesus took Peter, James, and John *up a mountain*. This is the sixth time in the Gospel that Jesus has ascended a mountain. There, at the top of the mountain, Jesus was transformed: "His face shone like the sun, and his clothes became dazzling white." Moses and Elijah then appeared and were talking with Jesus. Peter did not understand what was happening; consequently, his response –that he would make three dwellings there, one for Jesus, one for Moses, and one for Elijah –did not make sense. During the conversation between Jesus, Moses, and Elijah, a cloud overshadowed all of them, and the voice of God spoke: "This is my Son, the Beloved; with him I am well pleased; listen to him!"

What is the effect of this remarkable story? What does it accomplish? It draws us into a mystery that is both clear and foggy. It is a mystery of rock solid righteousness that we live through paradox: In following Christ, we will save our lives by losing them. We will take up the cross, only to find that it is the easiest yoke of all. We are called through the difficult, narrow door, only to find ourselves standing on rock solid ground. We are transformed on the rock of righteousness in the midst of our most stormy and even blinding of circumstances. Matthew makes this paradoxically clear immediately after Jesus feeds the five thousand (in chapter 14). Having sent his disciples across the Sea of Galilee on a boat, Jesus climbed a mountain, by himself, to pray. By evening, the disciples were having an awful time. They were being battled by wind and waves. What is remarkable is that at early morning, Jesus was walking to them on the stormy sea. Notice the mystery that Matthew conveys. The disciples were in the midst of the worst kind of storm, far from the shore. Jesus, on the other hand, was walking on the water *as if on solid ground*. Because the storm was so blinding, they at first didn't recognize Jesus and screamed in terror, "A ghost!" Jesus responded with words of assurance, calming their fear.

Finding courage, Peter asked Jesus to command Peter to walk to him on the water. When Jesus did so, Peter got out of the boat and started walking on the water. Peter enjoyed initial success, but when his attention turned from Jesus back to the storm, Peter, overcome with fear, began sinking: "Lord, save me!" Reaching out his hand, Jesus caught Peter: "You have little faith, why did you doubt?" Peter's challenge? He was still of at least two minds. This is because learning takes time. It's not an instantaneous occurrence. Peter was present to the storm. He was not yet planted firmly on the rock of righteousness in the midst of his storm. He was still at risk of sinking.

I think it worth noting the alacrity with which Matthew's Gospel moves us between the spiritual and material worlds. Matthew understands unbroken wholeness: He recognizes a connection between a transfigured world and a world that is material. Matthew shows us an unbroken wholeness of spiritual and material. I think that is why Christ must at times speak in paradox: Both realities are interwoven. This, I believe, is what J. Philip Newell meant when he said that on the Isle of Iona, the veil is thin: The community is actively engaged in a life of unbroken wholeness. In that sense, that little island is rock solid; it is a complete world. Listening for the heartbeat of God is a matter of life and the way we live it.

The difficulty, of course is to stay on solid ground in the midst of the stormy sea. For me the most important part of learning is review. I have to remind myself that the treasure that resides in the *gap* in the field of our imaginations is not the property of my imagination. The treasure is a gift: It comes from God; it belongs to God. It is accessible, but only as mystery. I have to return, again and again, to the memory of those first inklings, but I cannot remain in the past. Instead, I have to be fully engaged, completely present. In the words of Peter Senge and his colleagues, I have to let go, in order to let come. I have to embrace mystery so that I can find my footing. Having found my footing, I have to implement—to act, to allow the treasure to unfold within my own circumstances. Only then does living in righteousness and becoming a person of justice become a matter of habit—second nature. That is when we stand on the mountain at the intersection between time and place, the eternal present.

For Reflection

What is my experience with being distracted as opposed to being fully present?

_____

_____

_____

What is my experience with recognizing the connections between my interior world and the material world in which I live and move and have my being?

_____

_____

_____

What is my experience with instability versus having a solid place on which to stand?

_____

_____

_____

Who are the people in my life who are rock solid? What makes them so? What do I have to learn and gain from my interactions with them?

_____

_____

_____

What is my experience with injustice versus justice and righteousness?

_____

_____

_____

When in my life have I tried to satisfy my "appetites" instead of taking the right path? What have been the consequences?

_____

_____

_____

When in my life have I tried to impress others or been needlessly sensational?

_____

_____

_____

When in my life have I practiced self worship, or been "full of myself?" When have I taken myself too seriously?

_____

_____

_____

How have I been a stumbling block either to others or to myself?

_____

_____

_____

Why kinds of burdens do I carry? What would it take for me to pursue righteousness and to be lightly yoked?

_____

_____

What would it mean for me to save my life by losing it?

_____

_____

What would it take for me to plant myself firmly on rock?

_____

_____

_____

Chapter 6 — *the great teacher*

What is needed is to learn afresh, to observe, and to discover for ourselves the meaning of wholeness. Of course, we have to be cognizant of the teachings of the past, both Western and Eastern, but to imitate these teachings or to try to conform to them would have little value. For, as has been pointed out in this chapter, to develop new insight into fragmentation and wholeness requires a creative work even more difficult than that needed to make fundamental new discoveries in science or great and original works of art. It might in this context be said that one who is similar to Einstein in creativity is not the one who imitates Einstein's ideas, nor even the one who applies these ideas in new ways, rather, it is the one who learns from Einstein and then goes on to do something original, which is able to assimilate what is valid in Einstein's work and yet goes beyond this work in qualitative new ways. So what we have to do with regard to the great wisdom from the whole of the past, both in the East and in the West, is to assimilate it and to go on to new and original perception relevant to our present condition of life.

—DAVID BOHM, *Wholeness and the Implicate Order*

When Jesus saw the crowds, he went up the mountain; and after he sat down, his disciples came to him. Then he began to speak, and taught them.

—MATTHEW 5:1–2 (NRSV)

*H*ow does righteousness happen? To put it another way, how do people become just? Does taking the right path and doing the right thing come naturally? Even if we are partly inclined to do the right thing, especially in our treatment of others, I do not think that any of us, let alone all of us, is inclined to do the right thing all the time, especially as a matter of habit.

There is a wonderful fairy tale in the Brothers Grimm collection entitled, "Our Lady's Child." The story begins with a woodcutter and his wife, who were so poor that they could not afford to raise their beautiful daughter. As the woodcutter was working in the forest, the Virgin Mary appeared to him and offered to take the woodcutter's daughter to heaven and give her a secure upbringing. Much relieved, the concerned father consented.

In heaven, things could not have been better for the child. Her clothing was made of gold; she ate sugar cakes, drank sweet milk, and played with the little angels to her heart's content.

When the girl came into her fourteenth year, the Virgin Mary told the girl that she (Mary) needed to make a long trip. In her absence, she would entrust the girl with the thirteen keys of the kingdom. Mary granted the girl permission to open twelve of them, in order to behold the glory of all that was within. But the thirteenth was forbidden. Were she to open this door, the girl would bring nothing upon herself but misery.

Initially, she followed the Virgin Mary's instructions to the letter. Each day, the girl would open a new door and enjoy the splendor of a different apostle in all of his glory. On the thirteenth day, the girl was curious to know what lay behind the forbidden door. Sorely and predictably tempted, while also remembering Mary's command, even as the girl was aware of her weakening resolve, she said to the little angels, "I won't open the door entirely; I'll just take one small little peek."

The little angels were mortified: "No, no! That would be sin!! Do not do such a thing!!!" Alas, the girl was no angel; she was altogether human. She was also fourteen years old. When alone, she convinced herself that since no one was watching, she would satisfy her gnawing curiosity and desire without anyone ever knowing.

Taking the thirteenth key, the girl put it in the lock. When she then turned the key, the door sprang open of its own volition. There, the girl beheld the Holy Trinity in all of their glory. The vision filled her with such amazement that she reached with her finger to touch some of the light, which turned her finger all golden. This, of course, filled her with terror and dread. The girl slammed the door shut. How in heaven (for that is where she was) would she keep her transgression (for that is what her sin was) a secret? However much she would rub her finger, it remained ever golden.

When the Virgin Mary returned, she observed the girl's countenance, which was etched in guilt. Mary also noticed the golden finger. Knowing what the girl had done, Mary asked for a confession—three times. Three times, the girl refused. Three times, she lied.

Because the girl had done the one thing forbidden, she was exiled to the world from which she came. Moreover, because she lied in heaven, she lost her right to speak: Her voice was silenced.

On earth, the girl was discovered by a king. Because she was beautiful, the king married her. The girl's loss of speech led to problems: Every time she had a baby, the Virgin Mary would appear to her and ask if the queen would repent of her sin. Each time the queen refused. The consequent was that Mary would take the queen's newborn into heaven. The disappearance of the queen's babies led to the court's accusing the queen of cannibalism. Having no voice, the queen could offer neither defense nor explanation. The king finally consented to having his wife burned at the stake. But, at the fifty-ninth minute of the eleventh hour, the girl did the right thing:

She called out to the Virgin Mary and confessed to her wrongdoing. Immediately, the Virgin Mary doused the flames and delivered the queen from her punishment. In the end, king, queen, and restored children lived happily ever after (which is, after all, the final aim of the fairy tale).

One of the beauties of fairy tales is that they cut straight into the heart of a problem or dilemma. This fairy tale sets up the theme of The One Thing Forbidden. It helps us recognize that the inclination to do the right thing is not always first nature. We are all prone to self-interest and deception. All of us are capable of being up to no good at least some of the time. And when we do wrong, we suffer from a propensity to hide our actions.

Earlier in my life, I led retreats for young people. I would occasionally put a scenario in front of them: *We are in a large, multi-story cabin. This is our first time here. The counselors need some time to get organized, so we are going to go off for an hour and have a meeting. We know you to be responsible people. We are confident that you are trustworthy and won't get into trouble. So we'll leave you by yourselves for the next hour. Go anywhere you like. The only thing that we ask is that you not look into the left-hand closet on the second floor.* Having paused for a moment, I then ask the group, "How many of you will comply with my request and refrain from looking into the closet?" I have never had a group in which the majority said that they would comply. Moreover, even those who agreed to abide by the request took delight in the fact that someone else would open the forbidden door, insuring that everyone would know what lay behind.

I have also given my students a scenario: *The professor says, "I have to be gone for the next five minutes. A copy of tomorrow's exam is on the desk in the front of the room. Now, we are a Christian university, and I know that you have a well developed conscience and will not look at the exam. Just visit or study quietly while I am away. I'll be back in five minutes."* I know of no professor, myself included, who would do such a thing. Why? Because we all know that the temptation for a peek would be too great, a truth to which many of my students readily admit. The result of such circumstances is that the exam would not reflect an accurate assessment of the student's learning!

If the fairy tale of the Brothers Grimm reflects a truthful assessment of our humanity—if the temptation to transgression is inherent in all of us—then how do we become righteous? How does making the right choice and doing the right thing become a matter of habit? For if righteousness does not become habitual, and if we do not have the capacity and willingness for making the right choices—especially when no one else is watching—then we run the risk of hurting others and of failing to rise to the full stature of human excellence. Writers as diverse as Plato, Aristotle, Dante, Adam Smith, Fyodor Dostoevsky, and C. S. Lewis all recognized that for righteousness to become a matter of habit, something substantial must happen in the human heart. My head may know what is right, but if my sentiments aren't in line with my heart, doing what is right will be difficult and improbable. For Saint Augustine, one of the most important questions was, *how do we learn to love the right things in the right way?* This does not happen by accident. Loving the right things in the right way isn't first nature. We are not naturally just, at least not entirely so. We tend to concern ourselves more with self interest than with the interests of others. At the same time, we tend to want others to think highly of us. This being the case, for us to live well, a certain kind of learning is essential.

Matthew was one of the people who recognized that for us to become righteous as a matter of habit, a transformation of our consciousness is critical. What makes Matthew unique among the earliest of Christian writers was his recognition that the power by which God created the heavens and the earth and raised Jesus from the dead can also bring righteousness to fulfillment in the human heart and in a human community. He also devoted his considerable genius to the question of *how* we become righteous. To his undying credit, as well as our incalculable benefit, one of his insights was that *righteousness comes to fulfillment through education.* Becoming righteous involves great teaching and learning.

Matthew conveyed this insight in his portrayal of Jesus, and he developed his portrayal of Jesus through the *design* of his Gospel. One of the things that are obvious in Matthew's Gospel is the continuity that Matthew established between Jesus on the one hand and the Old Testament on the other. This first confronts us in the way Matthew begins his Gospel: The genealogy (Matthew 1:1–17) places Jesus at the climax of a lineage that begins with Abraham and passes through generations leading to David, the great king of Israel, and the Babylonian exile. The end of the genealogy portrays Jesus as the Messiah—the king of Israel—who brought the kingship of David to fulfillment. Matthew's characterization of Jesus as Messiah and Son of David is direct and straightforward.

Equally direct is Matthew's characterization of Jesus as Son of God. It is interesting to note that when Jesus was baptized in Mark's Gospel, the voice from heaven spoke to Jesus: "*You* are my Son." In Matthew's Gospel, the voice spoke not to Jesus, but to the bystanders: "*This* is my Son." Matthew is placing an emphasis on several identities and roles, which come together in Jesus. The Messiah (Christ) is the king of Israel. The Son of God is the one whom God delivers from captivity: The first time that God made reference to a son is in the book of Exodus. As God was instructing Moses with respect to his pivotal role in delivering the Hebrews from slavery and oppression, God said to Moses, "Go to Pharaoh and say, 'Israel is my firstborn son.'" God then delivered his firstborn son from slavery in Egypt by way of the Red Sea.

Jesus embodied both of these roles—Son of David (Messiah, or king) and Son of God (the One whom God delivered). This is one of the reasons that Matthew's genealogy passes first through David and then through the Babylonian exile: Just as David *was* Messiah, so Jesus *is now* the Messiah; and just as God *delivered* Judah from exile, so God *will deliver* Jesus through the resurrection.

Matthew then attributes a third identity to Jesus: the role of The Great Teacher. Matthew portrays Jesus as the New Moses. The way Matthew accomplishes this is a matter of literary genius. Matthew begins his narrative with Joseph, betrothed husband of Mary, who learned something of the mystery of Mary's pregnancy in a dream. Joseph's encountering this mystery *in a dream* associates him with an earlier Joseph who also came to the knowledge of God through dreams—Joseph the son of Jacob, whose extended story concludes the book of Genesis (chapters 37–50). Matthew wants us to recognize that just as the story of Joseph the dreamer in Genesis serves as a prelude to the story of Moses, so do the dreams of Joseph, betrothed husband of Mary, prepare the way for Jesus (Matthew 1–2). This sets up an entire series of associations, or analogical connections, between Jesus and Moses, with which Matthew unfolds his Gospel:

Just as Pharaoh felt threatened by Moses and the Israelites, so did King Herod feel threatened when the magi (the wise men) approached Herod in search of the child who was born king of the Jews.

Just as Pharaoh ordered the execution of Hebrew babies during the time period in which Moses was born, so also did Herod order the execution of the male children in Bethlehem when he learned of the birth of Jesus.

Just as the Israelites and Moses escaped the wrath of Pharaoh by fleeing from Egypt, so also did Jesus, Joseph, and Mary escape the wrath of Herod by fleeing from Bethlehem.

Just as Moses led the Israelites out of Egypt, so also did Joseph (after the death of Herod) bring Mary and Jesus out of Egypt, to their home in Nazareth.

Just as Moses led the Israelites out of Egypt across the dry riverbed of the Red Sea, so also did Jesus present himself at the Jordan for baptism.

Just as Moses led the Israelites into the wilderness, where they spent the next forty years, so also did the Spirit lead Jesus into the wilderness, where he spent forty days.

Just as Moses and the Israelites faced temptation in the wilderness, so also did Jesus face temptation from the Devil.

Just as Moses led the Israelites to a mountain (Sinai), which he climbed and received teachings from God (the Ten Commandments and the Covenant Code), so also did Jesus ascend a mountain, where he delivered the Sermon on the Mount (Mathew 5–7), through which Jesus interpreted and expanded on the teaching that Moses received from God.

Just as the story of Moses and the Exodus is *preceded* by the story of the ten plagues, so is Jesus's Sermon on the Mount *followed* by ten miracles (Matthew 8–9).

Just as Moses gave a series of blessings and curses as a part of his teaching, Jesus also integrates blessings and curses into his teaching (Matthew 5 and 23).

And just as Moses's final act was to ascend a mountain and to direct the Israelites to the Promise Land, so was Jesus's final act to take his disciples to a mountain in Galilee, where he directed them to all nations to baptize and to teach others all that Jesus has taught them (Matthew 28).

The ways in which Matthew makes connections between Jesus and Moses are ingenious: Instead of declaring, directly, that Jesus is the New Moses, the Great Teacher, Matthew presents Jesus inheriting, interpreting, reflecting, and fulfilling the teaching of Moses through the design of the Gospel. Matthew accomplished this by weaving and blending history, identity, narrative, interpretation, reflection, confrontation, call, and commission, all into one Gospel. In other words, Matthew miraculously blended these disparate realities into a miraculous whole. Matthew is the scribe who fits us for the kingdom of God by bringing from his treasure both the old and the new. The old includes Moses, the entire Exodus story, Abraham, David, Isaiah, Jeremiah, the Babylonian exile, and the like. The new includes Mark's understanding of Jesus, other stories that are not a part of the Gospel of Mark, the Sermon on the Mount, and Matthew's own questions and insights.

Matthew's recognition of the connection between Jesus and Moses could not be more significant. One of the most important insights that Matthew brought forth from his treasure involved the *means* by which we come to righteousness: education—teaching and learning. I have no doubt but that the other three Gospel writers understood the mystery of transformation. One of Matthew's unique contributions was his understanding of *the transformative nature of education as an essential means to the fulfillment of righteousness and justice.*

As with the other Gospels, Matthew built his Gospel on three major movements in the educational enterprise of transformation. The first movement involves *recognition*—learning to see with ever increasing clarity. Recognition includes giving attention both to the circumstances in which we live on the one hand and Matthew's Gospel on the other. This involves seeking to discover Matthew's insights into Jesus—his identity as Messiah, Son of God, and the Great Teacher. This also includes our learning to recognize the enduring impact of the presence of Christ in our world: *The same power by which God created the heavens and the earth and raised Christ from the dead brings righteousness to fulfillment in the human heart.* Put another way, Matthew's Gospel elevates righteousness in our imaginations in concert with the power by which God raised Christ from the dead. This is not a power from which we are alienated. The world that Christ and Matthew see is a world that is whole. When Christ looked at people, and when Matthew looked at Christ, they recognized the connections in which we live and move and have our being. We are not isolated selves. Transformation involves learning to recognize the complementary designs with which Matthew composed his Gospel, along with how we ourselves participate and live in those designs. Not only does Matthew portray Jesus as the Great Teacher, but Matthew also presents five major discourses that we can easily identify—the Sermon on the Mount (5:1–7:27), the Missionary Discourse (10:5–42), the Discourse of Parables (13:1–52), the Discourse on Discipleship (18:1–35), and the Apocalyptic Discourse (24:3–25:46). Inasmuch as Matthew wants us to recognize the associations between Jesus and Moses, he also wants us to see that there are connections between these five discourses and the Pentateuch (the first five books of the Bible). And in our reading and reflection, we can also recognize the connection that we have to each other in these discourses. Matthew makes it possible for us to see not only that Christ brought the Pentateuch to fulfillment, but also that Christ brings the Pentateuch to fulfillment in our hearts, lives, and circumstances.

Matthew does not, however, present a closed case and a finished product. He instead both invites and challenges us to embrace membership in the Kingdom of Heaven right where we are. Goodness, as Flannery O'Connor observed, is always something under construction. And we have no alibi for our failure to participate and respond. This is not, however, something we need to do in blind impulse, for a second critical movement in educational transformation involves *interpretation* and *reflection*. Before Jesus actually launches his disciples in serious ministry, he spends ample time teaching them. His teaching is detailed, patient, and sustained. Knowing and accepting his disciples' aptitudes, Jesus offers no crash course. This is not to say that his teachings lack urgency. He understands, however, that effective learning takes time. Moreover, effective teaching is concrete, set squarely on the solid ground of the circumstances in which we actually live. Jesus's teaching, in other words, is not esoteric head-tripping. No Ph.D. is required. Nor is the student absolved from giving Jesus's teaching a try in the school of hard knocks. The first large example that we have seen is the Sermon on the Mount (5:1–7:27), which we will address at greater length below. The contents are easy to understand. Implementation is another matter.

For better, for worse, Matthew understood and accepted that without *implementation*, there is no transformation. And by refusing to implement the fruit of our learning, we stubbornly persist in clinging to a stunted humanity. But like any great teacher, Jesus refuses to exempt himself from practicing what he preaches. Nor does he remain on the sidelines as spectator and Monday morning critic. Jesus doesn't lead by example so much as in engagement, inviting and urging us into complete membership in the wholeness of his undertakings.

In laying out ways in which Matthew portrays Jesus as the New Moses, the Great Teacher, I pointed to a certain twist in Matthew's plot: Whereas in the story of Moses, the Exodus and the events at Mount Sinai are preceded by ten plagues, in Matthew's Gospel, the Sermon on the Mount is followed by ten miracles (Matthew 8–9). There are several things that Matthew accomplishes from this insight. At the most obvious level, Matthew shows us that Jesus brings the accomplishments of Moses to fulfillment. Perhaps less obvious is how Jesus brings this about. The first plague that an Egyptian Pharaoh suffered is not from the book of Exodus, but from Genesis 12. This particular plague helps us understand not only what a plague is, but also the significance of Jesus's involvement with people who are plagued by their own debilitating maladies. The central figure in Genesis 12 is Abram (his name hasn't yet been changed to Abraham). Shortly after Abram and his wife Sarai arrived in Canaan, there was famine. In search of food, Abram took his wife Sarai to Egypt. On the way, Abram began to fear for his life. Sarai's beauty had something to do with this: Abram feared that the Egyptians, wanting Sarai, would kill Abram and seize possession of Sarai. In order to save his own skin, Abram asked Sarai to lie to the Egyptians and claim that Abram was her brother. To this, Sarai agreed. As Abram predicted, Sarai's beauty was not lost on the Egyptians, including the Pharaoh. To insure his own safety, Abram sold his wife Sarai into the Pharaoh's harem. The Pharaoh was then sexually intimate with Sarai, and the result of this interaction was a plague.

Many have found it odd, if not unjust, that the one who suffered the plague was the Pharaoh. I will not argue with those who want to hold Abram responsible. He is the one, after all, who instigated the entire mess. What I would like to focus on is the nature of the plague. The Pharaoh has engaged in adultery. He did so unwittingly, to be sure. But the perspective of the writers of Genesis is that Pharaoh's adultery is real. Moreover, he is in the position of power and dominance. *The plague is the symptom of a rupture in the field of the relationships* in which the Pharaoh, Sarai, and Abram are willingly involved. It is a fact that Abram and Sarai are husband and wife. It is a fact that marriage is an event that begins with the wedding. And it is a fact that the relationship between husband and wife is one of unbroken wholeness—complete interaction with each other and excluding sexual interaction with others. The Pharaoh's adultery with Sarai constitutes an assault on the person of Sarai and the field of Sarai's and Abram's marriage, regardless of the Pharaoh's unawareness of the situation.

This is all that we need to know to understand the significance of the ten miracles (Matthew 8–9) that immediately follow the Sermon on the Mount (5–7). Having concluded the Sermon, Jesus descended the mountain. A crowd followed Jesus, and he was approached by a leper. The leper treated Jesus with the greatest of respect: The leper knelt before Jesus. The leper then made a telling request: "If you choose, you can make me clean" (8:2). The leper's insight is remarkable in that he fully recognized that for Jesus's involvement with the leper to be authentic, Jesus must be free to give his consent. The choice must be entirely his. Jesus, in other words, was at liberty to walk away. At the same time, Jesus accepted that a situation called upon him to be fully engaged with the man making the request. The man was calling upon Jesus to be his best self, making the wisest decisions and choices possible. The Russian literary critic Mikhail Bakhtin tirelessly argued that to be human is to make mindful choices based on our best judgments. Moreover, there is no alibi that excuses our failure to do so. The times and places that call upon us for judgment and choice are often beyond our control. This means that being fully human involves acting and embodying. This is precisely what Jesus did with the leper. Jesus did not withdraw, decline, or flee the scene. He was fully present in that place at that time. Simply put, Jesus responded. The choice to respond was entirely his. By responding, Jesus accomplished several things simultaneously: He consented to allowing a relationship to come into being. The interaction between Jesus and the leper involved request, response, and relationship. My intuition says that the relationship is the most important of the three, for the relationship, coupled with Jesus's willingness to respond, elevated the leper's legitimacy and authenticity as a human being. According to Leviticus 13–14, lepers were "unclean." They were allowed no place in the legitimate community. Lepers were ostracized and lived in exile. Jesus not only engaged the leper willingly, but he also reached out and touched the leper. That direct, willing contact brought their relationship to fulfillment: It became a reality. At the same time, Jesus elevated the leper's dignity as a matter of public attention and awareness: The crowd that had just heard Jesus preach the Sermon on the Mount accompanied Jesus as he descended the mountain and encountered the leper.

The totality of the miracle established and legitimated an unbroken wholeness that involved the leper requesting, Jesus responding, and both fully participating in their relationship.

The same kind of thing happens in the second miracle. This request came to Jesus from a Gentile centurion on behalf of the centurion's servant. Here we have a centurion elevating the dignity of a slave, Jesus responding to the centurion's request, and the centurion responding to Jesus by elevating Jesus's dignity: "I am not worthy to have you come under my roof" (8:8). Is it not remarkable that the centurion would elevate both his slave and Jesus, making both foremost in the centurion's world?

At the same time, Jesus's acceptance and engagement with those who seek his help do not keep him from sustaining the implementation of relationships already established: His third miracle involves the mother-in-law of one of his foremost disciples, Peter.

Before continuing with the remaining seven miracles, Jesus directed his disciples to cross the Sea of Galilee. But right before their boarding the boat, a scribe approached Jesus, promising to follow him. Jesus's response to the man focuses on the necessity of genuine willingness: "Foxes have holes, and birds of the air have nests; but the Son of Man has nowhere to lay his head" (8:20). Another follower then says to Jesus, "Lord, first let me go and bury my father." Jesus's response seems harsh: "Follow me, and let the dead bury their own dead" (8:22). Jesus is clear that following him is not for the faint-hearted. More important is that the decision to follow Jesus is authentic because he recognizes the essentiality of the would-be follower's giving his or her consent freely. That is why Jesus offers the opportunity as an invitation, or call: There is no compulsory conscription. Following Jesus and engaging in ministry is a matter of willingness offered freely. This is not to suggest any lack of urgency or want of importance. At stake are matters of justice and righteousness. The paradox is that these essential values cannot be coerced.

Within the ten miracles, there is one exception to the issue of request and consent: the healing of the paralytic (9:2–8). In this episode, the paralytic was carried by others. It was in response to *their* faith that Jesus offered the paralytic the forgiveness of his sins. Jesus's action precipitated objection from some of the scribes, who accused him of blasphemy, a capital crime. Sacrifice at the temple was the conventional means for securing forgiveness. Jesus, in seeming contempt of the temple, offered forgiveness directly. What was not lost on Jesus was the cultural belief held by the scribes who challenged him: that one could not be healed without having first received the forgiveness of sins. When Jesus then healed the paralytic, Jesus was ratifying, *in their terms*, his authority to forgive sins.

It is of course possible that the paralytic lacked the capacity to make the request for forgiveness on his own behalf. What seems more certain is that the offer of forgiveness is inherently good: Forgiveness restores unbroken wholeness in relationships. This, I think, provides a sufficient basis on which we can understand something of the sense in which the ten miracles resolve problems embodied by the ten plagues. Whereas the plagues are symptoms of a rupture in the fabric, or field, of the world, Jesus's miracles re-constitute the world as unbroken wholeness. Jesus accomplishes this by engaging people in their most critical need. Jesus interacts with people with complete deliberation. Unlike the plagues, the wise and loving choices of Jesus bear the same power with which God will raise Jesus from the dead, a power which heals the rupture and re-establishes unbroken wholeness within the people he encounters and between people and the space in which they live and move and have their being. Put another way, Jesus's encounter, decisions, engagement with people, and choices in relationship re-establish connection and unbroken wholeness with what is seeking to emerge in their lives. In his interaction with people, Jesus elevates their value and sovereign dignity. Jesus restores and honors their humanity in the place where they live. Jesus connects them with the dignity of wholeness. Put another way still, Jesus's teaching and engagement effect deliverance from rupture, alienation, and isolation into the world of unbroken wholeness and communion—a value expressed in the "happily ever after" of the fairy tale. And yet, life is *not* finally a fairy tale. The possibility and opportunity for the unbroken wholeness of communion is eternal—an ever-present possibility and opportunity. Communion, however, is not a condition of passivity. We can be at rest in God and with each other, but the paradox is that this is a rest of active attentiveness, awareness, intention, and reflective choice.

For Reflection

What is my experience with loving the right things in the right way?

_____

_____

_____

In my own circumstances, where is life ruptured or plagued?

_____

_____

_____

As I have lived a life of learning, what role have justice and righteousness played? What have been the occasions when I have been the most reflective and learned to make better choices?

_____

_____

_____

What is the significance of Matthew's portraying Jesus as the Great Teacher?

_____

_____

_____

Why is it significant for Matthew to discover that the power by which God raised Christ from the dead also brings justice and righteousness to fulfillment here and now?

_____

_____

_____

In my life and world, how are justice and righteousness always under construction?

_____

_____

_____

What will it take for me to improve in implementing justice and righteousness? What circumstances in my own life are most in need?

_____

_____

_____

Who are the people in my life who are ostracized, living in "exile?" What would it take for me to serve justice?

_____

_____

_____

Where in my life do I tend to make excuses for inaction?

_____

_____

_____

Where do I need to be more mindful of the choices that I make? What will it take for me to do so? To ask this another way, what will it take for me to give consent to live fully, especially when justice and righteousness are at issue?

_____

_____

_____

Where life is ruptured, what steps can I take to re-establish unbroken wholeness?

_____

_____

_____

Chapter 7 ~
connecting the dots

If techniques cannot teach originality and creativity in art and science, how much less is it possible for them to enable us to 'discover the immeasurable'?

What man can *do is to give his full attention and creative energies to bring clarity and order into the totality of the field of measure. This involves, of course, not only the outward display of measure in terms of external units but also inward measure, as health of the body, moderation in action, and meditation, which gives insight into the measure of thought. This latter is particularly important because, as has been seen, the illusion that the self and the world are broken into fragments originates in the kind of thought that goes beyond its proper measure and confuses its own product with the same independent reality. To end this illusion requires insight, not only into the world as a whole, but also into how the instrument of thought is working. Such insight implies an original and creative act of perception into all aspects of life, mental and physical, both through the senses and through the mind, as this is perhaps the true meaning of meditation.*

—DAVID BOHM, *Wholeness and the Implicate Order*

In everything do to others as you would have them do to you; for this is the law and the prophets.

—JESUS, *in Matthew 7:12 (NRSV)*

83

We were having dinner. The earth began to shake. The sensation was one of rolling. It almost felt like we were riding a wave. I was in the eighth grade. I had experienced earthquakes before, but this got my attention. I was scared.

I thought the earthquake would never end. The entire house shook. Dishes in cupboards rattled. The dishes on the table where we were eating slid. The lamp that hung from the ceiling in the family room bounced and swayed. Finally, the earthquake stopped. The earth became calm again. It would be some time before my nerves followed.

Only one of us seemed unshaken—my father. Dad had nerves of concrete. He was an officer with the Sheriff's Department. As far as I could tell, Dad was fearless. He was the family rock. When there was genuine cause for panic, Dad was the island in the midst of the stormy sea.

Dad enlisted in the Navy at the age of seventeen, during World War II. He operated radar on a destroyer on the Pacific theater. When I was growing up, I had the impression that Dad never lost his radar: He always knew the way to solid ground. He grew up in Ocean Beach in San Diego. And because he spent so much of his life in the ocean, he was a strong swimmer. Consequently, Dad was also assigned to rescue pilots who had to bail out of their fighter planes. The Navy didn't have special training for this critical job. They simply relied on the competence that Dad developed as he swam in the ocean as a child. He was so good at this and so calm that one particular pilot, whom Dad had previously rescued, radioed to his aircraft carrier that he was going to have to ditch his plane. The pilot also requested that Jack Blackwell be summoned to rescue him. The pilot knew first-hand how calm and effective Dad was when it came to finding a safe solid place on which to stand.

Dad was never one to out his soul. He was respectful, thoughtful, and quiet. But shortly after his seventy-eighth birthday, I wanted to learn something about his strength of character, and I was able to persuade him to open up. I was not surprised to learn that his role model and inspiration was his mother. Grandma died when I was in the fifth grade, and I was grateful that Dad was willing to share. Hearing about her, I learned about Dad—what he most treasured.

Ethel Blackwell was a young mother who raised four children by herself. Dad's father was rarely home. The family was the poorest in Ocean Beach, and yet, their house was the place where all of the Ocean Beach kids liked to be. When they weren't at the ocean body surfing, they were at Grandma Blackwell's house. It was their safe harbor. Ethel Blackwell became a kind of second mom to every kid on the beach. Whenever kids hurt themselves, they'd go running to Ethel Blackwell.

Every Sunday, Dad's mother would take twenty kids to the Mission Beach Fun Zone. Each had his or her nickel to spend. And with Ethel leading the way, the group would walk from Ocean Beach to Mission Beach, enjoy the fun, and return on foot.

Ethel Blackwell liked everybody and associated with everybody— good and bad. She treated each one as the most important person in the world. The consequence for Dad was that the neighborhood bullies never picked on Dad or his siblings because of their respect for Dad's mother. The neighborhood *tough guy* loved Grandma's waffles. So whenever she was fixing waffles for breakfast, Grandma would tell Dad, or one of his siblings, to run over and get the boy so that he could have waffles with them.

Although they were the poorest family in the neighborhood, Grandma still gave away what she had to others. A boy in the neighborhood, who was also poor, once stole Dad's bathing suit and favorite shirt from her clothesline. Dad suspected the boy and investigated. Sure enough, Dad found out *who done it*. Dad dutifully reported this to Grandma. He told her that he was going to get his bathing suit and favorite shirt back, but

Grandma would hear nothing of it. She insisted that the boy be allowed to keep what he had stolen.

There was another poor boy with whom Dad grew up named Tom. Tom happened to be at Grandma's home on Thanksgiving. Grandma knew that Tom's family was too poor to afford a Thanksgiving turkey, so she gave him one of their big turkey legs. Over fifty years later, Dad attended his fiftieth high school reunion. Tom was there with his son. When he introduced his son to Dad, Tom said, "This is Jack. It was his mother who gave me the turkey leg."

At the same reunion, Dad saw another friend with whom he grew up. The first words out of the friend's mouth were, "Your mother was a saint." "This man had had a step mother, and she wasn't particularly nice to him," said Dad. Ethel Blackwell was the mother who had loved him.

Ethel Blackwell was a licensed vocational nurse. One December, a group of surgeons from San Diego were in Boston, attending a conference. They started talking about Ethel. They knew how poor she was. They were amazed at her kindness and character. One of them, a leading neurosurgeon, suggested that they do something for her for Christmas. Shortly before Christmas Eve, this surgeon handed Dad an envelope and told him to give it to his mother on Christmas morning. When she opened it, she discovered ten notes of appreciation from ten physicians. Each had a twenty dollar bill. As we say today, "That was a lot of money in those days."

When Grandma retired, the doctors called her into one of their meetings. They presented her a silver bowl in appreciation for her work and character. She was a solid rock and safe haven for more people than she would ever realize.

At Grandma's funeral, the flowers went around the entire perimeter of the mortuary chapel. The funeral director told Dad that these were the most flowers he had ever seen at a memorial service.

I personally know of only two times when my father has cried. At his retirement, a couple of tears dripped from his eyes as we all applauded. The one time that he let them flow was when Grandma died. She was Dad's rock. She was the bedrock of all of Ocean Beach. It was she who got into my father's soul. She is the one who embodied what he came to value the most. Grandma Blackwell is the reason that Dad was calm during the earthquake. Her example, her inspiration, and most important, her inescapable love, were a foundation of righteousness on which my father planted his feet.

My father was not a student of the Bible. And yet, there is one verse from the Bible that served as his focal point. Dad knew it as the Golden Rule: "Do unto others as you would have them do unto you." This is the rule by which Dad sought to live. I doubt that Dad could have told you that it comes from the Sermon on the Mount. But I know for certain that Dad tried to live it. The reason he has always been an unshakable rock is that he sought to live the Golden Rule.

The reason that my grandmother had such strong influence with my father was that the life she lived was compelling. My grandmother taught my father with words. But more important to him was the integrity and authenticity with which she lived. It was because the way she lived was compelling that her words had gravity.

This is one of the factors that make Jesus's words in the Gospel of Matthew compelling. Before the Sermon on the Mount, Jesus's largest single body of teaching, Jesus withstood a serious trial (Matthew 4). In the previous essay on "The Rock of Righteousness," we saw that Jesus faced three temptations: to satisfy his appetites (4:1–4), to make a spectacle of himself and become a celebrity (4:5–7), and to seize power to control (4:8–11). Were Jesus to succumb to these temptations he would do so by trampling God's teachings, putting God to the test, and selling his soul to the devil.

As my grandmother lived what she taught, Jesus taught what he lived. We encounter his first major teaching in the Sermon on the Mount (Matthew 5–7). When we look at the Sermon in the context of the entire Gospel of Matthew, we notice how closely it parallels the three episodes where Jesus faces the devil. Matthew recognized strong connections between the three tests in Matthew 4 and the Sermon. The Sermon on the Mount specifically addresses the kinds of tests that Jesus faced in the wilderness. There is, in other words, an unbroken wholeness between Jesus's facing the devil and the Sermon on the Mount.

Before we address the content of the Sermon, one more word concerning context is in order. When we look at Mark's Gospel, we notice that the first four disciples whom Jesus calls are fishermen—Peter, Andrew, James, and John. Jesus calls fishermen because following Jesus involves assisting him as he casts his net into the sea, lifting people from whatever abyss they are drowning in and placing them on solid ground. This is also true for Matthew's Gospel (4:18–22). At this point, Matthew makes his own contribution, offering his own insight. Matthew's Gospel more fully explores the nature of the solid ground. Matthew's metaphor for righteousness is rock or earth—having a solid place on which to stand. In Matthew's Gospel, Jesus calls his first four disciples immediately after he withstands his test before the devil in the wilderness. For Matthew, *following Jesus involves assisting him as he delivers people from the abyss of injustice by bringing righteousness to fulfillment in their lives.* Jesus then teaches in synagogues and heals the sick. This results in a large crowd that follows Jesus. It is at this point that Jesus ascends the mountain (echoing Moses climbing Mount Sinai) where Jesus preaches the Sermon on the Mount. This is the sermon that embodies the rock solid righteousness.

Much about the Sermon on the Mount is remarkable, not the least of which is its organization. This becomes clear when we see the Sermon in light of the three temptations that Jesus faced. Just as his first temptation was to satisfy his appetite at the expense of the teachings of God (*Turn these stones into bread.*), the first major block of teaching in the Sermon on the Mount addresses the Law of Moses, which was engraved in stone (Matthew 5:17–20). Just as the second temptation involves making a spectacle of self (*Jump off the pinnacle of the temple, and the angels will swoop down from heaven and catch you.*), the second major block of the Sermon portrays a life of anonymous goodness (6:1–18). And just as the third temptation involves selling one's soul to the devil for the purpose of manipulating and controlling others (*Worship me, and everything else is yours.*), the third major block of the sermon involves treasuring God and doing so absolutely (6:19–34). Still, from Matthew's perspective, this isn't enough. There is a final section to the Sermon on the Mount (7:1–28) in which *Jesus paints a clear picture of the life of righteousness.* This is the capstone of the Sermon on the Mount. This is where Jesus shows us how to live lives of righteousness and justice.

I would like to make an important observation about the significance of the way in which the Sermon on the Mount is organized. The organizational principle is not an exercise in mere intellectual sophistication. The organization of the Sermon addresses real life trials that all of us face that go to the heart of our humanity. *The Sermon on the Mount shows us ends that are worth living for, along with the means towards those ends.* There is yet another way to drive home the significance of the organization of these early chapters of Matthew's Gospel: We can see them in light of the first chapter of Genesis, where humans are created, male and female, in the image of God. This means that humans are not God, but there are significant ways in which we bear resemblance to God. There are aspects of our humanity that reflect the mystery and sovereign majesty of God—our human dignity. This observation is so significant that it draws forth questions of incalculable import: What does it mean to live in the image of God? How do we reflect the majesty of God? What are the most authentic images of human life and dignity? How do we rise to the full stature of our humanity? These are questions that Matthew's Gospel helps us with. The trials that Jesus faces portray tests that we ourselves face daily. And the understanding of God and the life of righteousness that the Sermon portrays offer an understanding of life and a way of living that bears the mystery of the image of God. It is hard to imagine anything more important.

Before getting to the main body of the Sermon, Jesus begins with a series of nine blessings, The Beatitudes. We have already seen the paradox in the Beatitudes (in the previous essay, *"Mind the Gap!"*). On the one hand, Jesus pronounces blessings—the presence of the life-spirit of God in the lives of people—the poor in spirit, those who mourn, the meek, those who hunger for righteousness, and so on. What we find surprising is the gap that exists between those who are blessed on the one hand, and their circumstances on the other. We learned that the power of God to raise Christ from the dead is what fills the gap between our spiritual poverty on the one hand and our being made fit for the kingdom of heaven—the kingdom of justice and righteousness—on the other. This raises the question, what can we do to welcome, embrace, and cooperate with the power of God? In the Sermon on the Mount, Matthew offers the teachings—the knowledge and wisdom—that we can take into our imaginations and store in our memories. The power of God works in connivance with the knowledge and wisdom of the Sermon on the Mount: When we place the contents of the Sermon in the gap between poverty of spirit and the kingdom of heaven, the power of God works in our souls through the Sermon to build righteousness in our dispositions and habits as we actively seek to implement justice in the world.

The invitation to seek and implement righteousness and justice in the world follows the Beatitudes—how it is that those who aspire to follow Christ carry these blessings: "You are the salt of the earth; but if salt has lost its taste, how can its saltiness be restored? It is no longer good for anything, but is thrown out and trampled under foot. You are the light of the world. A city built on a hill cannot be hid. No one after lighting a lamp puts it under the bushel basket, but on the lampstand, and it gives light to all in the house. In the same way, let your light shine before others, so that they may see your good works and give glory to your Father in heaven" (Matthew 5:13–16). The Sermon on the Mount is something that Christ teaches, to be sure. But the Sermon is no mere intellectual exercise. Jesus does give us much to chew on: We will recognize ourselves. And if we are willing to spend time in sustained reflection on the way in which the Sermon addresses our lives, we open ourselves to the possibility that the power of God that raised Christ from the dead can transform us, bringing us to the full stature of our humanity—the image of God. However, the faith that Matthew conveys is not a faith of mere reflection. Righteousness comes to fruition as we actively seek to implement justice—to do what is right by others.

I began this essay with a word about my father and the inspiration he received from his mother, Ethel Blackwell. I mentioned that one of the things that meant the most to him was that she befriended everyone. Regardless of whether a person was good or bad, Grandma Blackwell treated the person in front of her as the most important person in the world. This was the way Grandma Blackwell lived the Golden Rule.

If I might be so bold, this Golden Rule came to fruition in my father's treatment of others. One incident in particular stands out. When I was in my teenage years, the mother of one of my neighborhood buddies struggled with alcoholism. It was something that we were aware of, but it wasn't something we talked about. One evening, when my father was working in the County Jail, he looked up and noticed that this woman was being booked for driving under the influence of alcohol. My father's response was to duck out of there before she saw him. Dad didn't want our neighbor to suffer the indignity and humiliation of knowing that a neighbor knew the wrong she had done. Dad undoubtedly knew the pain that alcohol abuse brought upon a family: He, his mother, and siblings suffered for years. He knew first-hand the embarrassment caused and suffered. At the very least, Dad wanted to help this woman to save face. He wanted to do what little he could to help the family maintain whatever dignity they could.

For me, this is one of the most important things my father did for another human being. Dad not only took in what his mother taught, but he also tried to live with the same integrity with which she lived as well.

This is the kind of reality that Matthew portrayed.

For Reflection

Who are the people I have known whose lives are authentic? What has made them so?

_____

_____

_____

When I consider the people who have been the most authentic, what kinds of ends have they lived for? What has given their lives meaning?

_____

_____

_____

What might it mean for me to recognize that I am created in the image of God? How might I better embody the image of God?

_____

_____

_____

What is my life for? Why is this so?

_____

_____

_____

What ends are most worth living for? What will make life the most meaningful and rewarding both for others and for myself?

_____

_____

_____

What steps can I take to begin to rise to the full stature of my humanity?

_____

_____

_____

Chapter 8
in moral fulfillment

As has been seen, fragmentation originates in essence in the fixing of the insights forming our overall self-world view, which follows on our generally mechanical, routinized and habitual modes of thought about these matters. Because the primary reality goes beyond anything that can be contained in such fixed forms of measure, these insights must eventually cease to be adequate, and will thus give rise to various forms of unclarity or confusion. However, when the whole field of measure is open to original and creative insight, without any fixed limits or barriers, then our overall world views will cease to be rigid, and the whole field of measure will come into harmony, as fragmentation within it comes to an end. But original and creative insight within the whole field of measure is the action of the immeasurable. For when such insight occurs, the source cannot be within ideas already contained in the field of measure but rather has to be in the immeasurable, which contains the essential formative cause of all that happens in the field of measure. The measurable and the immeasurable are then in harmony and indeed one sees that they are but different ways of considering the one and undivided whole.

—DAVID BOHM, *Wholeness and the Implicate Order*

Do not think that I have come to abolish the law or the prophets; I have come not to abolish but to fulfill.

—JESUS, in Matthew 5:17 (*NRSV*)

*J*had always wanted to meet Dallas Willard. For years, I had been reading his books. Dr. Willard is Professor of Philosophy at the University of Southern California and Senior Fellow of the Trinity Forum in Washington D.C. All the people I know who read Willard have their favorite book. Mine is *Hearing God*. This is the book that helped me to see the importance of learning to recognize God's Voice so that my relationship to God may become conversational.

An opportunity to meet him came in October of 2003. Willard was one of the speakers at a conference at Point Loma Nazarene University in San Diego. The subject of the conference was the art of John Wesley, the eighteenth century priest of the Church of England and founder of the movement that became known as Methodists. Before Dr. Willard spoke, I happened to be standing next to him during the coffee hour. His personal warmth and humility touched my soul. I was all the more looking forward to his lecture.

I was stirred by what he said. I like it when lecturers begin with a question, because this has a way of drawing me into reflection. Willard began with a question: *What would it mean to live a life of moral fulfillment?* What would it mean to regard each episode of our lives as an opportunity to move towards, or to realize a kind of, fulfillment that made us morally complete?

He had my attention. I suddenly realized that I had never put the words *moral* and *fulfillment* together. I am a child of the 1960s. When I was growing up, morality was almost exclusively thought of as something merely restrictive, a list of dos and don'ts, with don'ts far outnumbering the dos! Morality, in other words, involved a lengthy list of *Thou shalt nots*. It was a *strictly a restrictive discipline.*

Dallas Willard challenged all of that. He was offering a different orientation: Why not think in terms of *moral fulfillment?* How does moral fulfillment come to fruition?

More than a list or prescription, the Sermon on the Mount urges us to ponder deeply—thoughtfully and long. When Jesus then comes to the main body of the Sermon, he says that his primary objective is *interpretation with an eye to implementation*: "Do not think that I have come to abolish the law or the prophets; I have not come to abolish but to *fulfill*" (5:17). Interpretation involves responding to and reflecting on what we read and hear, also bearing in mind the circumstances in which we find ourselves. His hope is that we will then act on our interpretation so as to bring it to fulfillment. Only then does interpretation become complete—as we fulfill the fruits of our reflection.

Jesus's subject matter that Jesus intends to bring to fulfillment is the law and teaching that came through Moses, especially the Ten Commandments, or Decalogue, found in Exodus 20 and Deuteronomy 5. Jesus interprets several of these laws, the first of which is the commandment against murder. Jesus's method of interpretation is to address the motive, the condition of the human heart that *leads* to murder—anger. I don't think that the anger that Jesus speaks of is the anger that we experience spontaneously and resolve in a constructive, peaceful manner. The type of anger Jesus speaks of is *willful wrath*—the kind that wishes harm to someone else.

Jesus's interpretation of the law moves immediately into steps that we can take to open ourselves to the grace of God: We can be mindful of those whom we have wronged, approach them, right the wrong, and ask for forgiveness. In other words, Jesus's interpretation of the law prohibiting murder immediately moves to a practice of *implementation in which the grace of God can work*: "I say to you that if you are angry with a brother or sister, you will be liable to judgment; and if you insult a brother or sister, you will be liable to the council; and if you say, 'You fool,' you will be liable to the hell of fire. So when you are offering your gift at the altar, if you remember that your brother or sister *has something against you*, leave your gift there before the altar and go; first be reconciled to your brother or sister, and *then* come and offer your gift" (Matthew 5:22–24). By taking responsibility for our behavior—by implementing Christ's interpretation and reflections—we open the gap in our hearts to the grace that transforms a person who wishes to take the right path (for that is what righteousness is), who wishes to be a peacemaker, but because of a poverty of spirit lacks the competence for doing what is right.

Having addressed murder and anger, Jesus then addresses the law prohibiting adultery. The same method of interpretation applies: Jesus is interested in the internalization of the law. In other words, he wants us to acquire the right motives and sentiments for loving the right people in the right way. Jesus hopes that our capacity for loving faithfully will become second nature. His understanding of adultery goes to the heart of the cause—lust. By looking at a person lustfully, we create the internal conditions that lead to adultery. Becoming possessed by lustful thoughts and sentiments, we commit adultery in our hearts. This leaves us spiritually disconnected and malformed. We see this in the implementation that Jesus prescribes as an antidote to lust: "If your right eye causes you to sin, tear it out and throw it away; it is better for you to lose one of your members than for your whole body to be thrown into hell. And if your right hand causes you to sin, cut it off and throw it away; it is better for you to lose one of your members than for your whole body to go into hell" (Matthew 5:29–30). Jesus's prescription for implementation gives cause for serious reflection: What would be the benefit of blinding ourselves by gouging out our eyes? And what would be the benefit to our humanity of cutting off our hands? By mutilating ourselves, we are committing grave sin against our bodies. In the same vein, by committing adultery, we in fact cut ourselves off from each other, shattering relationships, leaving fragments. Jesus's interpretation establishes an analogy for our reflection: Both adultery and lust leave us spiritually impoverished, fragmented, and malformed. On the other hand, by actively seeking and learning to love the right people in the right way, we grow into the full stature of our God-given humanity. We create communion.

We see this in Jesus's treatment of marriage (Matthew 5:31–32), the subject that follows adultery and lust. His call is for us to actively sustain a mutual commitment both to each other and to the marriage itself. To do otherwise is to adulterate both our spouse and our marriage. We can, however, ask one another, how best can I love you? How best can we honor our relationship as husband and wife? What will it take to place our marriage on solid ground? As a couple, how can we embody justice and righteousness? My wife Nancy and I find it helpful to ask, what will bring both of us the most delight, the most joy? What will it take for me to love so as to create the deepest of satisfaction? *If my goal is to interact with Nancy so as to bring her the greatest joy, as I actively love her, I recognize connections of unbroken wholeness, and my heart is transformed at the same time.* By seeking to understand how to love her, and by acting on that understanding, over time, I stand to enjoy growth as my capacity to love grows and becomes second nature—a matter of cultivated habit.

For Jesus, this is a matter of simple, direct truthfulness: "You have heard that it was said to those of ancient times, 'You shall not swear falsely, but carry out the vows you have made to the Lord.' But I say to you, do not swear at all, either by heaven, for it is the throne of God, or by the earth, for it is his footstool, or by Jerusalem, for it is the city of the great King. And do not swear by your head, for you cannot make one hair white or black. Let your word be 'Yes, Yes' or 'No, No'; anything more than this comes from the evil one" (Matthew 5:33–37).

Jesus is showing us at least two things. First, righteousness consists in truthfulness. Deception is antithetical to the right path. It causes fragmentation and brokenness in relationships. Moreover, when we become deceptive by nature, we build our lives on sand. The ground underneath is never secure. When we build our lives on sand, we position ourselves for our own destruction. Second, we can cultivate habits of righteousness by utilizing clear, straightforward speech. Why, for example, is a phrase such as *I swear to God, hope to die, stick a needle in my eye*, any better than simply speaking the direct truth? Do we risk impoverishing ourselves spiritually when we habitually preface our statements with self-initiated, convoluted, mock swearing-in ceremonies? And are we really any more convincing when, as a matter of practice, we tell others that what we are about to say represents the truth, the whole truth, and nothing but the truth? On the other hand, when we state matters simply, clearly, and with openness, we position ourselves to collaborate with God. That is moral fulfillment.

I have found my manner of speech to be one of the most effective (and I might add, difficult!) tools of change available. As early as the fourth grade (in 1962!), my classmates were experimenting with what we thought to be the most rebellious, colorful four letter words we could discover. Junior high, high school, and college simply engrained my habits of employing the most off-color speech I could devise. The result was that off-color and all too often inappropriate speech became a matter of habit.

I realize that I am not the only person who has struggled to uproot the 1960s from my disposition, but I am the only person who can take responsibility for John Blackwell! I can bemoan the difficulty of making appropriate speech a matter of habit, or I can make developing new habits a matter of moral fulfillment. I can recognize how powerful the human tongue is—both for good and for ill. I can recognize that my ways of talking have all too often been a symptom of my own spiritual impoverishment. And I can open myself to the power of God to bring righteousness to fulfillment in me as I seek to open myself to God's power through my efforts to employ words that are truthful and wise. I have not found this to be an easy journey, nor have I achieved perfection. But it is a journey in which the rewards exceed the challenges and difficulties.

Jesus next turns to the difficult issues of how we relate to our enemies. Both of his teachings are difficult at best. And I have met few people who liked Jesus's interpretation of the issue of retribution: "You have heard that it was said, 'An eye for an eye and a tooth for a tooth.' But I say to you, Do not resist an evildoer. But if anyone strikes you on the right cheek, turn the other also; and if anyone wants to sue you and take your coat, give your cloak as well; and if anyone forces you to go one mile, go also the second mile. Give to anyone who begs from you, and do not refuse anyone who wants to borrow from you" (Matthew 5:38–42).

Years ago, I was in a seminar with Dr. Walter Wink. Having researched this passage extensively, he concluded that this text has less to do with fist fighting, and more to do with humiliation: In the time of Jesus, when people came to blows, custom required them to use the right hand. According to Wink, there were fines for using the left hand because it was used for unclean work. For example, a Jew ate only with his right hand. Striking someone on the left cheek with the right hand would involve not a punch, but a backhand slap. And a backhand slap has less to do with violence and more to do with an insult. In other words, the purpose of the backhand slap is degradation; it is meant to humiliate one's enemy.

This raises an interesting question: What is the significance of responding by offering the left cheek? It is difficult to slap the left cheek with a right backhand. In other words, by offering the left cheek instead of retaliating, I first stand for my own dignity as a human being. I also position myself so as to make it difficult, if not impossible, for my opponent to continue to degrade me. I may even place my opponent in the position of looking like a fool.

I confess to liking Walter Wink's interpretation: It is fascinating in its reflection of Jesus's ingenuity. But even if Wink were not entirely correct in his reading of the Sermon on the Mount, Jesus's teaching is remarkable for the self control that implementation calls upon. Jesus's interpretation of the laws of retribution requires nothing short of goodness aforethought. Jesus doesn't settle for mindless, knee-jerk retaliation. He calls us to sustained reflection on the long term consequences of our response to conflict. He calls us to reflect on the possible outcomes, along with the consequences both for our opponents and for ourselves. He is showing us that when our response is as measured, thoughtful, and constructive as possible, we position ourselves for the power of God to operate in and through us for an outcome that is of benefit both to our opponent and to our own character.

One of my treasures is an autographed 1966 photograph that Bob Fitch made of Dr. Martin Luther King Jr. Dr. King is standing at his desk. A photograph of Gandhi is on the wall to the right of Dr. King. To this day, the genius of both Gandhi and King fills me with awe. Both sought to implement Jesus's teaching in the most hostile of circumstances. Implementation required the greatest of commitment and self control. Their methods of active nonviolent resistance were designed to accomplish several things together. First, they were designed to stand for the dignity of the person implementing nonviolent resistance. Second, they were designed to appeal directly to the dignity and conscience of the opponent. Third, they were designed to appeal to the dignity and conscience of the world at large. And fourth, they were designed to expose the evil of injustice as it was confronted by a response that embodied righteousness at its best. The righteousness that Gandhi and King led people to implement was one of the most constructive responses that modern history has witnessed. They have shown us the presence of the power of God in the most difficult of circumstances.

Jesus's teaching on retribution doesn't stop with turning the other cheek. For him, moral fulfillment involves loving our enemies. Jesus recognizes that loving our enemies is the most difficult kind of love: We can have little motivation to do so. Loving our enemies is an act of supreme will: It is premeditated and completely voluntary. Because of this, when we decide and choose to love our enemies and establish unbroken wholeness, we position ourselves to receive the power by which God raised Christ from the dead, which is in connivance with our efforts. Our willingness, coupled with God's power, fills the gap of our loathing for our enemies. The fruit of our efforts and collaboration with God is moral fulfillment.

Later in his Gospel, Matthew shows us that both the decision to love and the decision to refuse to love have consequences (Matthew 18:21–35). This is the first long narrative parable that is unique to Matthew's Gospel— the Parable of the Unforgiving Servant. The storyline is straightforward. A king is settling accounts with his servants. He discovers one who owes him ten thousand talents. This is an enormous sum of money: One talent equals ten thousand denarii. A denarius equals one day's wage: If we think in terms of minimum salary for an eight hour shift, we get the idea of a denarius. This means that the servant owes the king one hundred million day's wages.

There is no way that the servant can repay the king, so the king orders that the servant be sold into slavery and that payment be made. However, the sale of the servant, along with his wife and children, would barely add up to one talent, let alone ten thousand. The servant responds by begging for time to put together the ten thousand talents (which, incidentally, would be impossible). Suddenly and spontaneously, the king feels pity for the servant and forgives the entire debt. The servant is completely free!

This very servant, who has just been forgiven an enormous sum of money, leaving the presence of the king, happens to meet a fellow servant, who owes him one hundred denarii—one millionth what he himself has just been forgiven. Seizing his fellow servant by the throat, the forgiven servant demands immediate repayment. The fellow servant pleads for time, which is identical to the first servant's response to the king. The first servant, however, refuses. Instead, he has the fellow servant incarcerated for his inability to make immediate restitution.

There are other slaves present who witness the entire situation. They are troubled over the behavior of the slave who has been forgiven, so they report what they have witnessed to the king. When the king learns of the behavior of the unforgiving servant, he is livid. He summons the slave whom he has forgiven, and after lambasting him for refusing to offer the kind of forgiveness that he himself has received, the king delivers him to the jailers until he should repay his original entire debt.

In the Sermon on the Mount, when Jesus compels us to love our enemies, we are wont to find Jesus to be impossibly demanding. Loving our enemies can be one of the most difficult things imaginable. When Matthew includes the Parable of the Unforgiving Servant in his Gospel, he offers us enormous help: The word "parable" means *to place alongside*. A parable is a story that we can place alongside other situations or circumstances and then reflect on them so as to see more clearly. Jesus's parable shows us that when we refuse to love, when we refuse to offer grace that we have received, we imprison and isolate ourselves from the whole world. But when we actually forgive our enemies and actively love them, we free ourselves as we free them. So doing, we position ourselves for moral fulfillment: We become partners in creating a whole new world.

Not long after hearing Dallas Willard, I had the privilege of meeting two other important Christian leaders from the Los Angeles area—Dr. Cecil "Chip" Murray and the Reverend Leonard Jackson, senior and associate pastors of First African Methodist Episcopal Church of Los Angeles. Dr. Murray has been senior pastor for twenty-seven years. Rev. Jackson, in addition to his duties at the church, is chaplain for the Los Angeles Police Department. The senior

pastor of First United Methodist Church of San Diego, Dr. Jim Standiford,
had invited Murray and Jackson to come to San Diego to preach. Following
our morning services, I had the honor of taking them to lunch, along with my
colleagues. Our conversation was warm and searching. We wanted to glean all
that we could that would help us to become a better church.

I was particularly interested in Rev. Jackson's work as a police chaplain,
inasmuch as my father had served the San Diego County Sheriff's Department,
and my daughter Jaime is a prosecutor. I have always held a place of honor for
law enforcement officers in my heart. I knew that for years the chief of police
in Los Angeles had faced the daunting challenge of weeding out corruption
from within his own department. Nothing is more poisonous to a city or
more discouraging to a hard-working officer than corruption from within. I
took the opportunity to ask Leonard Jackson how the current chief of police
was doing with this problem. His answer inspired me.

Rev. Jackson said that at the heart of the chief's efforts to eliminate
corruption was his building of morale. He treats his officers and their families
as utterly precious. Jackson told us of a recent incident that involved an
accident. One of the officers was injured. In response to the situation, the
chief ordered the department helicopter to pick up the family of the injured
officer and to bring them to him so that they could be together.

I found the chief's action remarkable. He recognized that moral
fulfillment within his department went hand-in-glove with group morale.
Righteousness is *both* a personal matter *and* a community enterprise,
involving unbroken wholeness in relationships. Moral fulfillment within
the community cannot happen when we are isolated from each other.
The chief recognized that the implementation of righteousness has to
do with embracing personal limits and making the right choices for the
common good. But he also recognized that this could best happen within
a climate of mutual love and support. For him, the implementation of
righteousness began by communicating to his department that each and

every department member *and their families* count. They are precious. They are invaluable. The implementation of righteousness began with the recognition of the incalculable worth of each person in God's world.

I couldn't help but notice how Dallas Willard's lecture and Leonard Jackson's story complement each other. *The fulfillment of righteousness is both deeply personal and completely communal.* The demands of righteousness can be daunting. But when we create a community of love and forgiveness, the foundations are in place for moral fulfillment—both in its personal and interpersonal aspects. The two, in fact, cannot be separated.

For Reflection

Where have I experienced (and perhaps even caused) moral rupture or bankruptcy?

_____

_____

_____

In my life, where have I allowed anger to get the better of me? Are there people with whom I need to be reconciled? What would it take for me to make reconciliation more likely?

_____

_____

_____

What kinds of thoughts obsess me? What kinds of things and people do I lust after? What are the consequences of this lust—both for others and myself? What would it take for me to change, to be transformed, and for me to rise to the full stature of my humanity?

_____

_____

_____

What kinds of words do I use? What is my manner of speech? What does this say about the kind of person I am?

_____

_____

_____

How am I when it comes to honesty and truth? Where am I deceitful? What will it take for me to become truthful?

_____

_____

_____

How can I interact with others so as to bring greater fulfillment both to them and to the relationship?

_____

_____

_____

When I face conflict, how can I stand for the dignity of both my opponent and myself? Why might it be important to do so?

_____

_____

_____

Where is forgiveness most needed in my life? What are the consequences of my willingness to forgive or my refusal to forgive?

_____

_____

_____

Where are relationships broken? What can I do to bring about wholeness? What steps will I take?

_____

_____

_____

Chapter 9

"you are your secrets"

When such harmony prevails, man can then not only have insight into the meaning of wholeness but, what is much more significant, he can realize the truth of this insight in every phase and aspect of his life.

—DAVID BOHM, *Wholeness and the Implicate Order*

Beware of practicing your piety before others in order to be seen by them; for then you have no reward from your Father in heaven. So whenever you give alms, do not sound a trumpet before you, as the hypocrites do in the synagogues and in the streets, so that they may be praised by others. Truly I tell you, they have received their reward. But when you give alms, do not let your left hand know what your right hand is doing, so that your alms may be done in secret; and your Father who sees in secret will reward you.

—JESUS, in Matthew 6:1–4 (*NRSV*)

His name was Orval Hobart Mowrer. Mowrer did what I suspect I might have done had my mother named me Orval Hobart: He became a therapist. Specifically, Mowrer practiced psychoanalysis. And in the early 1950s, Mowrer was suffering with a bad case of vocational burnout. Psychoanalysis involves lots of words. It can also involve lots of sessions before the patient enjoys significant results. Mowrer became discouraged. His experience was that the quantity of words spoken in psychoanalysis seemed to be inversely proportional to the results of healing produced. Simply put, Mowrer was finding the form of therapy he was using to be ineffective. You might even say that he was having a midlife crisis.

The year was 1954. Mowrer's daughter had been trying to persuade her father to read one of the novels of Lloyd Douglas. Douglas was a popular writer. One of his best loved novels was turned into a movie: *The Robe*. Mowrer dismissed his daughter's suggestion that he read Lloyd Douglas. Mowrer's prejudice was that Douglas's novels were sentimental rubbish. When I first read about the exchange between Mowrer and his daughter, I could understand his reaction: My maternal grandmother loved reading Douglas, and she was incredibly sentimental. But Mowrer's burnout so weakened his resistance that he relented to his daughter's suggestion and read *Magnificent Obsession*.

In the novel, a young physician, Dr. Wayne Hudson, is struggling with failure and depression. Then Hudson discovers a "secret" that transforms his life. He learns that most people live "depleted" lives—lives void of vitality, creativity, enthusiasm, and joy—because whenever they perform a good deed, they make certain that others find out about it. In other words, they call attention to themselves. They boast of their accomplishments. They position themselves under the most flattering stage lighting.

The problem with letting others know of our good works is that by telling others, instead of storing the credit for that deed in my soul, I spend the credit for the immediate satisfaction of personal recognition.

When Nancy and I served a congregation in Las Vegas, we did our grocery shopping at Vons. This particular Vons had fourteen video poker machines which were mostly used by women on Social Security: When they received their Social Security checks, they would cash them and gamble the money away in these poker machines. What they did was to spend the money on instant gratification. Once they did so, the money was gone. Similarly, what Mowrer discovered from *Magnificent Obsession* was the insight that when a person does something good for someone else and then makes certain that others learn of the good deed, the person spends the credit for the good work on the immediate, short-term satisfaction of personal recognition instead of secretly storing the credit in his or her soul.

The complement to this situation is what happens when we do something wrong or mean-spirited: We try to make certain that no one else finds out. We hide our evil actions. We conceal them. By keeping our mean behavior secret, we store the "credit" for our meanness in our souls.

It was in reading *Magnificent Obsession* that Mowrer discovered an insight: "You are your secrets." The meaning is straightforward: If I want to know the condition of my soul, the contents of my character, or the kind of person I am becoming, I can simply look at the secrets I keep. Secrets come to make up a significant part of our character. If I do something evil and keep that secret, I become more evil. If, on the other hand, I do something good, and if I then boast about my deed, the goodness never has the opportunity to settle in my soul. In other words, if I do something good, but do so with motive—to look good, to receive adulation, to be admired by others—I squander the credit, and the credit is gone, just like that. The inner vitality I might otherwise have gained evaporates. I become morally depleted and unfulfilled.

Mowrer knew that Douglas found inspiration for this insight in the New Testament. It didn't take him long to discover the place: It is in the sixth chapter of Matthew, in the Sermon on the Mount. This is where Jesus addresses our desire for fame and celebrity, our propensity for trying to impress others (Jesus's second temptation—to jump off the pinnacle of the temple to be rescued by angels). Jesus addresses our craving for recognition by pointing to the manner by which we help people: "Beware of practicing your piety before others in order to be seen by them; for then you have no reward in heaven. So whenever you give alms, do not sound a trumpet before you, as the hypocrites do in the synagogues and in the streets, so that they may be praised by others. Truly I tell you, they have received their reward. But when you give alms, do not let your left hand know what your right hand is doing, so that your alms may be done in secret; and your Father who sees in secret will reward you" (Matthew 6:1–4).

When Mowrer reflected on this teaching from the Sermon on the Mount, he thought about it in relation to his practice of psychotherapy. This led Mowrer to try a new therapeutic method: confession of wrongdoing and anonymous good works. So Mowrer tried an experiment with his next patient, a young man. At the end of his session, Mowrer suggested an assignment, which consisted of two complementary tasks: The young man was first to find two people whom he trusted, who would keep his confidence, and make a clean breast of all the wrong he had done. Through personal confession, he was to unload his meanness and sins. He was no longer to keep his wrongdoing a secret. In the second part of the assignment, instead of coming to his next therapy session, he was to take the money he would otherwise pay for the session and do something good for someone. The one condition of the good deed was that he was to tell no one. Mowrer told the young man to keep his goodness a secret, to do his good works anonymously.

The young man was intrigued by the challenge. He not only followed Mowrer's prescription, but he did so with zeal. When the young man returned for his next therapy session, he seemed to be a new man. He reported to Mowrer what he learned from his experience—that his own soul had been bankrupt. He had been keeping the consequences for wrongdoing in his soul, and he had been spending the credit for any good deed by telling the whole world. But by confessing his wrong-doing, he was ridding himself of evil, and by doing good anonymously, he was becoming changed as a person.

What Mowrer accomplished was to recognize and to reflect on an important insight from the Sermon on the Mount. From his reflections, Mowrer developed a therapeutic insight of his own—that his patient might find inner strength by implementing Christ's teaching. The young man not only did so; he learned through his subsequent reflection on the changes he was implementing. This brought about his transformation. He enjoyed greater autonomy and personal freedom. The young man recognized that he was being transformed on the inside as he implemented change in his behavior and interaction with others. The young man enjoyed a personally rewarding measure of moral fulfillment as he actively changed the secrets he kept. So doing, he became more fully human, enjoying a greater awareness of his own dignity. His personal satisfaction was self-authenticating: It rang true.

When Jesus comes to the main body of the Sermon on the Mount, he tells us that the purpose of the Sermon is to bring the teaching of Moses to fulfillment (Matthew 5:17–20). To achieve this goal, Jesus then directs our attention to important parts of the Law of Moses (5:21–48). When we looked at this part of the Sermon in the previous essay, we focused on the ways in which it addressed the problem that Jesus faced in his first test—the temptation to turn stones into bread (4:1–4), allowing appetites to undermine righteousness. Jesus continues his description of the narrow path to fulfillment by addressing our thirst to be highly thought of (4:5–7). His instructions are straightforward (6:1–18): Instead of doing good works to draw attention to ourselves, we are not only to do goodness in secret, but we are not even to let our right hand know what our left hand is doing. We help no one when we use piety to gain recognition. Prayer isn't about eloquence, nor is it about showing off. Prayer is about interacting with God in humility and reverence: "Whenever you pray, go into your room and shut the door and pray to your Father who is in secret; and your Father who sees in secret will reward you" (6:6).

In lieu of convoluted, self-aggrandizing prayer, Jesus recommends The Lord's Prayer (Matthew 6:9–13). The prayer is simple, but it is also packed with meaning. We live in prayerfulness when we hold God's name as holy. We seek the world of God's sovereignty by recognizing that God's will, which is always being done in heaven, is something that we can implement on earth. This includes asking for daily bread for all (give *us* our daily bread). It includes asking for forgiveness *to the degree that we are willing to forgive others* (in the previous essay, we looked at the consequences of the unwillingness to forgive in Jesus's Parable of the Unforgiving Servant). And it includes asking God to deliver us from the kinds of tests that Jesus faced in his encounter with the devil in Matthew 4.

When we look at the Sermon on the Mount in its entirety, we can recognize a paradox: On the one hand, Jesus says, "You are the light of the world.…. Let your light shine before others, so that they may see your good works and give glory to your Father in heaven" (Matthew 5:14, 16). On the other hand, Jesus teaches us to do our good works in secret (Matthew 6:1). How do we make sense of this seeming contradiction? Jesus's parable, The Workers in the Vineyard (20:1–16), complements his teaching on letting our light shine while doing our good works anonymously. The storyline of the parable is simple and straightforward: The owner of the vineyard needs laborers. He therefore goes out early one morning, finds people willing to work, and hires them. He repeats this action several times. He first goes out at six a.m., then at nine a.m., then at twelve noon, then at three p.m., and finally at five p.m. Each time, he finds people who are unemployed and hires them. He also gives his employees the promise to pay them what is right.

At six p.m., the end of the workday, the owner of the vineyard directs his steward to pay his laborers, beginning with those who worked one hour and ending with those who worked for twelve. Those who worked for one hour receive an entire day's wage. So also do those who worked for three, six, and nine hours. Those who worked a twelve hour shift observe what is happening and begin to think that the owner of the vineyard will give them a bonus! But like the others, they receive one day's wage—neither more nor less.

The twelve hour workers are incensed and express outrage to their employer. The owner of the vineyard, however, argues that he is free to do what he chooses with his own money. He also questions them for begrudging his generosity.

When I teach this parable, it is not unusual for me to encounter resistance. I have known people to flat-out object to the parable, agreeing with those who worked twelve hours that the owner of the vineyard is not treating them fairly.

I do not presume to understand everything about this parable. I can also sympathize with the people who raise objections. I would, however, like to make one or two observations. They will pertain to the paradox of letting our light shine while keeping our good works a secret. There is a degree of anonymity in the owner's willingness to pay all of his employees an equal wage: He never offers a satisfactory explanation. These employees do not think highly of their employer. They are angry. The owner, instead of offering explanation, keeps his reasons to himself. This said, we can still find good reason for the owner's actions, especially when we look at Matthew's Gospel in its entirety (especially his last parable in 25:31– 46). *The owner of the vineyard makes hospitality a part of his economy.* In the Middle East, hospitality was a matter of sacred duty. If a traveler sought food and shelter, the responsibility to satisfy the person's legitimate needs was a matter of protocol. The institution of hospitality recognized the link between a person's vulnerability and dignity. The institution of hospitality required treating the stranger as guest. In the Parable of the Workers in the Vineyard, the focus of the owner is on the dignity and need of his employees—without reference to the time that they have been in his employment. First and last, his employees are not the objects of labor; they are people. For the employer to season employment with hospitality, without specifying his reasons, is for him to let his light shine as he does his good works in a fair measure of anonymity. He refuses to engage in a popularity contest by flaunting his motives. Nevertheless, we may recognize something of his reasoning by reading the parable and placing his behavior in the larger context of Matthew's Gospel as a whole.

The Sermon on the Mount doesn't end with instructions about anonymous good works. There are additional matters that Jesus deals with, not the least of which is the temptation to sell our souls for the opportunity to manipulate, control, and coerce—"Again, the devil took him to a very high mountain and showed him all the kingdoms of the world and their splendor and he said to him, 'All these I will give you, if you will fall down and worship me'" (Matthew 4:8–9). Jesus understood that the desire to control others is the ultimate self-aggrandizement. This form of self-worship involves selling our souls to the devil.

Jesus's response to the devil is that we are to worship God solely—first and last (Matthew 4:10). In the third major section of the Sermon on the Mount (6:19–34), Jesus shows us how to live our lives in worship of God. He first needles us for our propensity of becoming human pack rats—piling up too much stuff! I am embarrassed to write that I myself am guilty of this. When I travel, by the time I pack my laptop, cords, phone, phone cords, iPod, cords, ear phone, electric shaver, cords, Kindle, and cords, my carry-on looks like a miniature Electronics Store. And on my last trip, my suitcase weighed over fifty pounds because I had taken far more books than I could possibly read on a single journey. I began to wonder what this says about my humanity, especially when I read the words, "Do not store up for yourselves treasures on earth, where moth and rust consume and where thieves break in and steal; but store up for yourselves treasures in heaven, where neither moth nor rust consumes and where thieves do not break in and steal" (6:19–20). The reason that Jesus gives is elegantly simple: "Where your treasure is, there will your heart be also."

I find it fascinating that Jesus then talks about the eye as the *lamp of our bodies* (6:22). This raises the question of focus: On what do I set my sights? What do I insist on looking at? Do I have obsessions? If so, what are they? And how do I regard the things that I see? As I take them into my consciousness, what do they do to me? How do they shape my character, the kind of person I am becoming? What happens when the objects of my focus become a part of my secret inner self? Worse, what happens if they fill my soul with darkness?

The poet Dante reflected on this reality in "Purgatory 10" of his epic, *The Divine Comedy*. This is the place where souls are purged of their propensity for self-aggrandizement, manipulation, and control. The penitents first encounter great art, the subject of which is humility. Being purged of the Deadly Sin of Pride first involves a sustained gaze on art that portrays people who treasure God. The artistic examples of others who treasure God lay the groundwork for our doing likewise. It is as we come to treasure God that our bodies are filled with light.

Jesus complements the issue of what we focus on by relating it to what (and whom!) we serve: "No one can serve two masters; for a slave will either hate the one and love the other, or be devoted to the one and despise the other. You cannot serve God and wealth" (Matthew 6:24). Why is this so? The answer is straightforward: *Where your treasure is, there will your heart be also* (6:21). It turns out that the things we habitually see and the stuff we hoard are intimately related. They also have everything to do with the contents of our character and the nature of our relationships.

I composed the following story in an effort to convey something of the insight that righteousness is both personal and corporal. It is not finally an either/or reality, but a both/and.

She looked up from the ornate sofa on which she customarily sat. There, in the middle of her living room, stood the angel of death. From beneath his black hood, she could see his old ochre face. Reaching out his bony hand in her direction, he addressed the old woman. "It is your time."

"So much do you know!" was her answer. "You neither knocked at the door of my house, nor are you welcome. Get out, before you become the victim of my displeasure!" Her words were as uncompromising as they were firm.

Accustomed to being merely feared, the Angel of Death departed—for the time being.

The entire house which she owned was filled with riches that overwhelmed calculation. And the presence of the Angel of Death hammered into her awareness that her riches had sat idle, benefiting no one, and offering her little by means of any real pleasure. So the rich widow arose from the sofa to which she was ever near and resolved to make an inheritance of her wealth.

She began by making a journey throughout the village. Her pilgrimage was shamefully modest by most standards—a mere trip around the neighborhood. But for the widow, it was like traveling to the four corners of the earth.

The purpose of her journey was to invite her neighbors to her home. It was the first invitation she had ever made. And this represented the first contact that most in her village had had with the old woman. By the time her journey was complete, no one was lacking an invitation. Neither did anyone refuse.

The invitations were to a meal at the wealthy widow's home. Each gathering of widow and neighbor consisted of three parts—a request that the neighbor share something of his or her story, a meal of delicious food and warm conversation and tea, during which the widow would give to her neighbor a portion of her estate according to her neighbor's need.

As the sun set on the eve of the conclusion of her last gathering, the widow sat for one last time on her sofa, which had now become her deathbed. There was one last knock at the door. Before answering, the Widow took a last look at the room in which she sat, which, appropriately, had been relieved of the burden of its riches. Having so paused, she lifted her voice and spoke her final words: "You may come in now. I am ready."

The Angel of Death opened the door of the widow's home and entered. This time, his face looked much less unfriendly. "I will make your journey easy." Ever so respectfully, and with kindness aforethought, he received her hand.

Their journey was not entirely unlike the one she had made around her own village neighborhood. But at its conclusion, the widow was not sure whether they had traveled for hundreds of thousands of years over the seemingly infinite deep, or if they completed their journey in the twinkling of an eye.

Upon their arrival, the Angel of Death led the woman into a large Hall. As they entered, the host of heaven stood. The Angel of Death led the woman down the immeasurable aisle to the Dock of the Accused. The Angel of Death then took his place among the host.

In silence, the Judge entered the Hall of Judgment. All the host of heaven fell to their faces. The Judge took his place at the Bench. All of the host were then seated. The Judge then looked at the woman, who stood on the

Dock of the Accused. Without diverting his eyes, the Judge spoke: "The Messenger of the Court will bear testimony to the life of the one who stands in judgment."

"What testimony will you hear, O Lord?"

"The testimony that was given at her funeral. How was the woman remembered?"

On a Witness Stand in front of the Bench lay an open book. Moving to the Witness Stand, the Messenger of the Court turned several pages. Having found his place, the Messenger of the Court read to all assembled the following words from the Book of Life.

"On the day following the death of the accused, the people of the village gathered at their house of worship. The service began with the singing of a hymn. This was executed with difficulty. Many were unable to sing, for they were crying.

"At the conclusion of the hymn all were seated, heads bowed. After several minutes of silence, a woman rose and spoke. "Because of her generosity, I was able to give my children their first hot meal in weeks."

She was followed by a man: "When she reached out to us, I was able, finally, to quit drinking."

Another man: "Her generosity completely changed me. Before, I was such a nasty person. Through her, something happened."

A twelve year old boy: "My mom took money that the woman gave to her and bought me a new pair of shoes. Now my feet aren't cold, and the shoes don't have holes in them."

A young woman: When she reached out to us, my husband stopped yelling at the kids and stopped beating me. She filled him with such confidence that he has begun to work again."

The Messenger of the Court continued to read testimonies that lasted for over an hour. He ended with these words: "At the conclusion of the service, the congregation stood and sang the Doxology. The service was attended by everyone in the village.

For an eternity that quilted the Hall of Judgment, the Judge and host of heaven were silent. The Judge sat in contemplation with head bowed. When he finally spoke, he did not lift his head. He addressed the woman haltingly, giving her the impression of One who had been broken.

"To the accused on the Dock, I speak words that are treasured from the foundation of the Created World Order. Come, O Blessed, and inherit the kingdom that is prepared for you. For I was hungry, and you gave me food. I was naked, and you clothed me. I was sick, and you visited me. I was a stranger, and you welcomed me. I was dead, and you gave me your life."

And now, the Judge spoke with even greater difficulty. "I have but one word to speak to you. It is the most important word that is spoken in both heaven and earth."

It was then that the Judge lifted his head, and the woman and all the Host of Heaven saw why he spoke with such difficulty. His eyes were filled with tears. The Judge was crying. "Thank you. Thanks to you from the Heart of God."

And then, to the Host of Heaven: "Never has there been more Gladness than belongs to Heaven and Earth on this day. Salvation is complete in the life of this soul."

For Reflection

What kinds of secrets do I keep? What are the consequences of this reality, especially for the way that I live and the impact I have on others?

_____

_____

_____

In what ways do I call attention to myself? What are the consequences of this behavior for my own spirit and character? What are the consequences for my relationships with others?

_____

_____

_____

What role does forgiveness play in my life? What changes do I need to make? What are the potential consequences, especially for justice and righteousness?

_____

_____

_____

When it comes to doing good things for others, what might it mean for me to maintain anonymity?

_____

_____

_____

How might I make hospitality a part of my life? What are the consequences of my willingness to offer or withhold hospitality?

_____

_____

_____

What is my experience with self aggrandizement—either in others or in me? What are the consequences?

_____

_____

_____

What do I spend time looking at? With what realities do I fill my mind? What are the consequences?

_____

_____

_____

How generous is my spirit? What steps am I willing to take to grow in my generosity?

_____

_____

_____

Chapter 10
the mystery of matthew's numbers

So fragmentation is in essence a confusion around the question of difference and sameness (or one-ness), but the clear perception of these categories is necessary in every phase of life. To be confused about what is different and what is not, is to be confused about everything. *Thus, it is not an accident that our fragmentary form of thought is leading to such a widespread range of crises, social, political, economic, ecological, psychological, etc., in the individual and in society as a whole. Such a mode of thought implies unending development of chaotic and meaningless conflict, in which the energies of all tend to be lost by movements that are antagonistic or else at cross-purposes.*

—DAVID BOHM, *Wholeness and the Implicate Order*

When he came to the other side, to the country of the Gadarenes, two demoniacs coming out of the tombs met him.

—MATTHEW 8:28 (*NRSV*)

As Jesus went on from there, two blind men followed him, crying loudly, "Have mercy on us, Son of David!"

—MATTHEW 9:27 (*NRSV*)

After the Sabbath, as the first day of the week was dawning, Mary Magdelene and the other Mary went to see the tomb.

—MATTHEW 28:1 (*NRSV*)

rom time to time, a student will come to my office prior to the beginning of a semester. The purpose will be to check out my approach to the interpretation of Scripture. It is unusual for the student to confront me directly. But it is not unusual for the student to try to entrap me, without first announcing the game, which is *Gotcha!* I cannot say that I look forward to these encounters. I have deep reverence for the Bible. On the day that I composed this final essay, I was sitting at breakfast in St. Deiniol's Library in Wales. A husband and wife joined our table for breakfast. The man asked me what I was working on, and I told him, "The Gospel of Matthew." His response intrigued me: "Isn't it interesting that we have these little books that make up our Bible, and after two thousand years, people are still writing about these very books!" It is interesting indeed.

Interesting as the Bible is (and I never cease to be fascinated), the Bible is important to me for many reasons, some of which are beyond description. In the category of "beyond description" is the area of mystery. The fact that something is mystery means that it is not something that can be measured, analyzed, or completely (if even partially) described. And I happen to be one who believes that great literature doesn't explain mystery; it draws us close to mystery. This by itself would make the Bible singularly important to me. And yet, there is more, though I will mention only one factor here: The Gospel of Matthew, among (many) other things, not only deals in the virtues of justice and righteousness, but it is itself a vehicle for the conveyance and cultivation of justice and righteousness. As I write, the world is still involved in wars that are at the very least messy, the world economy is limping at best, and the quality of public discourse and dialogue is all too often myopic, if not non-existent. Americans still fight over a health care plan with reckless polarity, never having taken the time for a thoughtful public searching to the question, as human beings and as

Americans, what do we owe each other in terms of an adequate measure of medical care? I am under no illusion that people will cease to think in terms of self interest, but I am still enough of an optimist to believe that our leaders can engage us in this kind of dialogue and debate and that people can rise to the occasion. Moreover, I believe that the Gospel of Matthew can help greatly because he places these questions squarely before us. We cannot read Matthew thoughtfully (and in its whole) and avoid questions of doing right by each other. I love all of the classes that I teach, but my classes in New and Old Testament are the last I would give up willingly. The matters that they address are far too important to lay aside.

One of the consequences of this approach is that I try on the one hand to read the Bible honestly and in the context of each book in and of itself. Among other things, this means that I am not a de-bunker. There are places in the Bible that taken at face value make contradictory claims. I don't pretend that the differences aren't there, but neither do I believe that, for reasons I will explain, they discredit the Bible.

Even so, I am not afraid of the student who comes to my office prior to the start of a semester to see if I'm the real goods. That my students want to know if I am a believer is more than fair. And they have a right to know that I love what I teach and do not use my soapbox to destroy their faith. But it is not uncommon for the student who wants to take me for a test drive to want a warranty that states that I believe in the "infallibility of Scripture." Sometimes I can refrain from pointing out that infallibility is a claim occasionally made by the Pope, but is not in the Scriptures. And sometimes I can resist asking if the student actually intends the adjective "inerrant" rather than "infallible." Yes, that is what the student actually means. If I then ask what the student means by "inerrant," the student will typically say that the Bible is the Word of God and is completely free from error. If I am in a particularly feisty mood and not overly-impatient to get back to what I was doing prior to the student's importunity, I might ask one or two questions. One goes something like this: "What is it that would cause people to assert that the Bible is 'inerrant?'" Because my second question is a bit more charitable (however slightly), I sometimes begin with it because it actually helps in the answering of the first: "When you compare what the four Gospel writers report in their accounts of the resurrection of Jesus from the dead, what do you notice?" If truth be told, I want these students in my class. One reason has to do with my admiration for people who believe with firm zeal. For the most part, these are students who engage the study of the Bible fully: They read their assignments ahead of time, come to class, and engage in the discussion. Moreover, many of the students who want to check me out so that they know what they're getting into are more than willing to learn. I had one student who asked, point blank, if I teach correct theology. I actually thought about saying No so that I could see where this took the conversation, but what I actually said was, "Tell me what correct theology I should teach!" To his credit, he had the humility to say, "I guess I don't really know." I not only complimented and thanked him for his honesty; but I assured him that my goal was for all of us to engage in an honest reading of the Bible and to discover together what we have to learn.

I wish that I could say that I am always successful in achieving that goal. I am happy with many a class session, but there are some that I wish I could do over. If my observations are correct, there are differences in the Gospels, and it doesn't require a college degree to see them (what it takes to deny them is not the subject of this book!). In the classroom, I will occasionally challenge my students with an exercise. I will have them read and compare the empty tomb stories in the four Gospels (Matthew 28, Mark 16, Luke 24, and John 20). I may even ask them to do so in groups. When we re-group, the students weigh in. I serve as scribe. What do they notice? *On their own*, they discover that in Matthew's Gospel, *two* women go to the tomb. In Mark, *three* women go to the tomb. In Luke, *three named* women, plus *additional unnamed women,* go to the tomb. And in John, *one* woman goes to the tomb. My students also notice differences in what the women find there. In Matthew, there is *one angel* outside the tomb. In Mark, there is *one young man* inside the tomb. In Luke, there are *two men* inside the tomb. And in John, there are *two angels* inside the tomb. John's Gospel has a race to the tomb that the first three Gospels do not have. Jesus appears at the tomb in Matthew and John. Jesus appears later in Luke (but not at the tomb). In Mark, the risen Jesus doesn't make an appearance. Finally, in Matthew alone, there is an earthquake that accompanies the resurrection.

This is the time in our discussion when a student will sometimes make a statement that goes something like this: "We all know that when there's a traffic accident, different witnesses will report different things. Their testimony won't match one hundred percent." When this happens in class, I want to respond with the greatest of respect and care. I want the student to reflect on how the issue of different witnesses with different testimony squares with an assertion that Scripture—because it was written by God— is inerrant. Would not God remove the errors? I believe that this is an important challenge that is completely appropriate for the study of the Bible in a university setting. Still, I care about my students; I admire their faith; and I am not interested in "blowing their doors off." Moreover, it is not unusual that I have students who want to do their own de-bunking of the Bible. It is as important to me to help them to see the insights that the Gospels convey as it is with those who would pretend that there are no differences to come to terms with. Moreover, most of my students become puzzled over these differences because most are aware of the standing of the Bible throughout the last two thousand years of history. Some wonder if these differences somehow discredit the Gospels. I do not find this to be the case. Instead, differences help us to recognize the insights that individual Gospel writers place before us.

Matthew is the perfect Gospel for learning to see important insights that differences convey. Like Mark, Matthew has a story of an exorcism (compare Mark 5:1–20 with Matthew 8:28—9:1). When we place these two stories side-by-side, we notice that Jesus exorcises *one* demoniac in Mark, but *two* in Matthew. The same is true when Jesus heals the blind (compare 8:22–26 with Matthew 9:27–31, and Mark 10:46–52 with Matthew 20:29–34): Whereas in Mark, Jesus heals *one* blind man, in Matthew, he heals *two*. What kinds of realities is Matthew showing us? His initial insight may have to do with the observation that the blindness provoked by evil is all too easily multiplied. This is certainly one reality that confronts all of us—our entire world. Whole nations are capable of being snookered from time to time. Matthew also wants us to recognize those occasions in which we willingly blind ourselves. For both Mark and Matthew, their second stories of the healing of the blind immediately follow a request that James and John be allowed to sit at the right and left hand of Jesus when he sits on his throne in glory. This request is completely self-aggrandizing. It seems that Matthew wants us to recognize that the *two* brothers, James and John, are blinded by their pride, or ambition. Does Matthew also want us to see the association between the self-aggrandizement of these *two* brothers on the one hand and the *two* demoniacs on the other? Does Matthew want us to see that the desire of James and John for self-aggrandizement is just plain wrong?

There are more examples where the number two comes into play. In Matthew 4:18–22, when Jesus calls his first disciples, he calls them in pairs. This is also true in Mark's Gospel, but Matthew—apparently using Mark as his source—emphasizes the number two. In chapter 10, Matthew also names the disciples in pairs. In chapter 21, Jesus sends two disciples into Jerusalem to prepare the Passover (similar to Mark), but in Matthew there are also *two* animals, a donkey and a colt, where in Mark there is only one. In 21:28–32, Matthew alone features a parable of *two* sons (this is different from Luke's Parable of the Prodigal Son). And in Matthew's apocalyptic discourse, there are *two* in the field, but one is left, and *two* grinding meal together, but one is left (24:40–41).

Then there are large narrative parables that are unique to Matthew. We have already seen the Parable of the Unforgiving Servant (18:23–34). This parable features *two* slaves, whose situations are analogous to each other. And in the Parable of the Workers in the Vineyard (20:1–16), there are *two* kinds of laborers—those who work a complete shift and are unhappy with their pay, and those who work fewer hours, but are happy. In the Parable of the Wedding Banquet (22:1–14), there are *twice two* kinds of people: those who respond to the invitation versus those who do not, and the ones who are properly attired, as opposed to the one who is not. And then in the climatic parables, there are *two* types of bridesmaids, wise and foolish (25:1–13), *two* types of investors (25:14–30), those who invest versus the one who refuses, and *two* types of people who stand in judgment: those who feed the hungry, clothe the naked, and welcome the stranger, versus those who do not (25:31–46).

What are we to make of this emphasis on the number two? In one sense, it comes as no surprise that for Matthew, the climatic story is the Resurrection of Jesus from the Dead (28:1–15). And when we take note of the similarities and differences between Matthew's account on the one hand, and Mark's, Luke's, and John's on the other, we can see that in Matthew alone, *two* women go to the empty tomb. This provides an essential clue into Matthew's insights: Matthew invites us to see that the blindness and evil embodied in the story of the exorcism of the *two* demoniacs and the *two* stories of the healing of the *two* blind men are dealt with and resolved by what the *two* women at the tomb bear witness to: The power by which God delivered Jesus from the tomb is the same power by which God delivers us from evil, blindness, and all of the ramifications that follow. The power by which God raised Christ from the dead is what brings justice and righteousness to fulfillment. And the reason that there are two women is that we experience this fulfillment not just personally, but in communion with others. This is the power in which we forgive those who owe us something or who sin against us. This is the power that makes it possible for us to be generous with others. This is the power that helps us to discern and to take the narrow road of righteousness. This is the power that accompanies our willingness to do the drudgery of preparation (securing oil for our lamps). This is the power in which we take risks—not reckless risks, necessarily, but risks all the same. And this is the power in which we recognize Christ in the hungry, the naked, the homeless, the stranger, and the prisoner, and then respond with hospitality and love. The issue is not that Matthew (or Mark, Luke, and John) couldn't count. The issue isn't myopic witnesses at a car wreck. The issue for Matthew involves learning to recognize how we come to build on rock and stand in righteousness.

For the fulfillment of justice and righteousness, the mystery of the number two is essential: It is not a needless statement of the obvious to observe that in Matthew's Gospel, righteousness comes to fruition in relationships. When Jesus says, "For where two or three are gathered in my name, I am there among them," this revelation immediately follows his statement, "If two of you agree on earth about anything you ask, it will be done for you by my Father in heaven" (18:19–20). I don't for a minute believe that Jesus intends to bless anything and everything two people contrive. On the contrary, by the time we reach the eighteenth chapter of the Gospel of Matthew, it is clear that earth, among other things, is Matthew's metaphor for rock solid righteousness—having firm footing. More subtle, but every bit as important, is Matthew's insight that justice and righteousness happen in and through relationships. That is where we find the world of righteousness. Dostoevsky wrote, "Where two or more are gathered, there is a whole world." The gap in the soul of those of us who know ourselves to be spiritually impoverished is filled by the power of God by which God raised Christ from the dead—the treasure hidden in the tomb. But this does not happen in isolation; it happens in relationships where we seek to implement justice. Righteousness is not something we pursue in isolation; it's something we seek and do together. That is why Jesus observed that a house divided cannot stand (12:22).

At the heart of Matthew's genius is his ability to make righteousness visible. Like the virtues of faith, hope and love, or the fruit of the spirit—love, joy, peace, patience, kindness, generosity, faithfulness, gentleness, and self-control—righteousness is not a material reality. But it is a self-evident reality nonetheless: It is something that we embody in our interaction with each other, especially when what is at issue is justice (another self-evident, non-material reality). Moreover, righteousness is an essential good for personal and social well-being and participation in the Kingdom of God. Matthew composed his Gospel on the insight that Christ transforms our consciousness for righteousness in and through our engagement with each other. Relationships have an inherent value: They are priceless.

Through the Gospel of Matthew, we come to share events with Christ where righteousness and justice are of supreme value—or to use Matthew's word, a treasure. Embracing the vision of the Gospel of Matthew, we come to recognize in our relationships with others the presence of the treasure of righteousness, the person of Christ. The Gospel makes us witnesses to Christ being responsible *to* others *for* others. As we observe Christ responding there and then, we gain the capacity to respond here and now.

There is more: The Gospel of Matthew makes us witnesses to Christ as he brings together disparate voices thought to be hopelessly incompatible. The Gospel embodies a series of events where people are compelled to make deeply reflective critical judgments that embrace the dignity, openness, and possibility of being in communion with one another. The Gospel shows us that all of us have a stake, and the stakes could not be higher because what is at stake is life itself: *Life is a treasure.* Its value is mystery. And it is in the presence of this mystery that we make choices with forethought and so doing become more fully human, aware that a common dignity binds us together.

The Gospel of Matthew capacitates us to pay attention to the concrete lives we are living right here and right now, to discern the best path, and to take it. And how do we accomplish this difficult task? Through imagination. Imagination is the gift of God. It is what distinguishes us as humans: We are created in the *image* of God, and it is in and through imagination that God creates and re-creates the world. Imagination is a treasure. It is more robust than fantasy. Fantasy is involuntary and subject to the illusions of enchantment, but imagination is wed to the human will, which is not only voluntary, but which can insist on clarity. It can also involve hard work, drudgery, and frustration. But the perseverance of imagination is usually rewarded with inspiration.

Imagination is the seat of insight.

Imagination is the sitting room where we welcome the Gospel and provide hospitality and fellowship and begin the search for answers.

Imagination is an interior laboratory where we measure and analyze. It is also the inner chapel where we come to know the immeasurable.

Imagination is the archive of memory. It is also the pub where we talk, cajole, weigh, debate, accept, or reject new (and sometimes old) ideas.

Imagination is the waiting room where we pause from the impulse of knee-jerk reactions or rash spontaneity. It is the scale on which we weigh our ideas so as to act with adequate measure.

Imagination is the water's edge of reflection. It is also the studio in which we exercise sovereign creativity, which is ours alone.

Imagination is the engineering firm that determines the parameters of the road best travelled. It is the accounting firm that audits our judgment.

Incarcerated in a concentration camp, Victor Frankl discovered imagination to be the last space in which we alone are sovereign. It is the birthright that guarantees our capacity to seek, to know, to embrace, and to implement the power by which God raised Christ from the dead. Through imagination and imagination alone, we know the treasure hidden in the field.

Matthew's Gospel capacitates our imaginations to attend, to intend, and to live well. This becomes likely when we seek to invest the same curiosity, wonder, and imagination that Matthew did as he composed his Gospel. The Gospel of Matthew can't be reduced to a single beatitude, parable, or even story of the resurrection. What the Gospel of Matthew has accomplished instead is the opportunity to bring us into communion with Christ and with one another as our imaginations participate in the unbroken wholeness of the Gospel. That communion is a process in which we are at rest in the Mystery, the flow of unbroken wholeness, which brings circumstances and opportunities to us, or us to those circumstances and opportunities, where it becomes our responsibility as humans to act upon reflection, to make the wisest choices of which we are capable, and then to act on those choices as we fulfill being humans ever in the flow of righteousness.

For Reflection

What are some of the most important insights I have gained from the Gospel of Matthew? What impact do these insights make on my life—the ways in which I think, reflect, and live?

_____

_____

_____

There are many ways in which Matthew makes connections throughout his Gospel. What might this imply about the kinds of connections we can make with the Gospel on the one hand and with the many facets of our lives on the other?

_____

_____

_____

The last parable in Matthew is the Parable of the Last Judgment. What is the relationship of this parable to the virtue of hospitality? What might hospitality have to do with justice and righteousness?

_____

_____

_____

What role does risk taking play in my life? How might I characterize my propensity for taking risks? Is my behavior typically too risky, perhaps even reckless? Am I too conservative and over protective when it comes to risks? What kinds of risks might I be taking to ensure justice and righteousness?

_____

_____

_____

In what sense are justice and righteousness a rock solid reality or a matter of personal preference? What might the consequences be of either situation?

_____

_____

_____

What might the bringing of disparate voices to the table of dialogue have to do with effecting justice and righteousness?

_____

_____

_____

What role does imagination play in the growth of justice and righteousness?

_____

_____

_____

How important is it that I learn to rest in mystery? What kinds of steps can I take to do so?

_____

_____

_____

What steps am I willing to take to participate in and to implement unbroken wholeness?

_____

_____

_____

About the Author

JOHN N. BLACKWELL IS VICE PRESIDENT for Student Development and Dean of the Chapel at Kansas Wesleyan University. For over thirty years, John has also served as speaker and retreat leader for people of all ages, both in the United States and Europe.

John received his education at San Diego State University, Claremont School of Theology, and Arizona State University, where he earned a Ph.D. in anthropology. This is his seventh book.

John and his wife, Nancy, make their home in Salina, Kansas. They have two adult children, Jaime and David, and a daughter-in-law, Chynnene. John enjoys reading, writing, teaching, music, travel, and kite flying.

Acknowledgments

IT IS ALWAYS A PLEASURE TO THANK those who are supportive of one's efforts to study and to write.

I begin with the talented design team at Morgan James Publishing for their creativity, insight, and spirit. Working with David Hancock and his competent staff is always a pleasure.

I am also grateful to Fletcher Lamkin, President of Kansas Wesleyan University. My work at Kansas Wesleyan is made doubly sweet because of the value that President Lamkin and my colleagues place on study, reflection, and writing. Because of the people of Kansas Wesleyan University, I am one grateful, happy camper.

I am also grateful to Peter Francis, Warden of St. Deiniol's Library in Wales. St. Deiniol's is a residential library. For me, it's a writer's paradise. This is so not only because of the unique setting of St. Deiniol's; it is also because of Peter, his family, and staff. They practice the best of hospitality while conducting themselves in a completely professional manner. They embody both the warmth and competence to which they aspire.

Molly Vetter, Minister of Justice at First United Methodist Church in San Diego, once told me that she would like someday to write a foreword to one of my books. Owing to her passion for justice, I thought her the perfect person. I am grateful to Molly for her friendship, witness, and willingness to introduce this book.

Shirley Leggett is a good friend who gives me seemingly unlimited assistance in the production of our books. I always benefit from both her sharp eye (she's a great proofreader) and feedback. I know of no person who exceeds Shirley's enthusiasm for the learning enterprise. This is what makes her such a great teacher.

I am honored to dedicate this book to two friends, Ben and Kathee Christensen. For years, I have known them through their work with the San Diego School of Christian Studies. I have had the pleasure of spending many an hour in dialogue with Ben and Kathee over ideas from the Gospel of Matthew. I treasure the insights I have gained from their remarkable intelligence, thoughtfulness, and humor.

Finally, I never tire of thanking my wife, Nancy, and our children, Jaime and David, and our daughter-in-law Chynnene. They are the treasures with whom I live and move and have my being. Owing to their grace, life is never boring in the Blackwell household.

Books
BY JOHN BLACKWELL

Reflections—Thoughts Worth Pondering One Moment at a Time (New York: Morgan James, 2009)

A Whole New World—the Gospel of Mark: Great Insights into Transformation and Togetherness. (New York: Morgan James, 2007)

A Whole New World—the Gospel of John: Great Insights into Transformation and Fulfillment. (New York: Morgan James, 2006)

Pride: Overcoming the First Deadly Sin (New York: Crossroad, 2006)

The Noonday Demon (New York: Crossroad, 2004)

The Passion as Story—The Gospel of Mark (Fortress Press, 1986, second printing 2010)

BUY A SHARE OF THE FUTURE IN YOUR COMMUNITY

These certificates make great holiday, graduation and birthday gifts that can be personalized with the recipient's name. The cost of one S.H.A.R.E. or one square foot is $54.17. The personalized certificate is suitable for framing and will state the number of shares purchased and the amount of each share, as well as the recipient's name. The home that you participate in "building" will last for many years and will continue to grow in value.

Here is a sample SHARE certificate:

YES, I WOULD LIKE TO HELP!

*I support the work that Habitat for Humanity does and I want to be part of the excitement! As a donor, I will receive periodic updates on your construction activities but, more importantly, I know my gift will help a family in our community realize the dream of homeownership. **I would like to SHARE in your efforts against substandard housing in my community!** (Please print below)*

PLEASE SEND ME _____ SHARES at $54.17 EACH = $ $_____

In Honor Of: _____

Occasion: (Circle One)   HOLIDAY   BIRTHDAY   ANNIVERSARY

OTHER: _____

Address of Recipient: _____

Gift From: _____ *Donor Address:* _____

Donor Email: _____

I AM ENCLOSING A CHECK FOR $ $_____ PAYABLE TO HABITAT FOR HUMANITY <u>OR</u> PLEASE CHARGE MY VISA OR MASTERCARD *(CIRCLE ONE)*

Card Number _____ Expiration Date: _____

Name as it appears on Credit Card _____ Charge Amount $ _____

Signature _____

Billing Address _____

Telephone # Day _____ Eve _____

PLEASE NOTE: Your contribution is tax-deductible to the fullest extent allowed by law.
Habitat for Humanity • P.O. Box 1443 • Newport News, VA 23601 • 757-596-5553
www.HelpHabitatforHumanity.org